Clipper Studies in the Theatre
ISSN 0748-237X
Number Ten

Doors into the Play
A Few Practical Keys for Theatricians

by

Sydney H. Spayde
with Douglas A. Mackey

R. REGINALD
The Borgo Press
San Bernardino, California □ MCMXCIII

THE BORGO PRESS
Publishers Since 1975
Post Office Box 2845
San Bernardino, CA 92406
United States of America

*   *   *   *   *   *   *

Library of Congress Cataloging-in-Publication Data

Spayde, Sydney H., 1907-
  Doors into the play : a few practical keys for theatricians / by Sydney H.
Spayde with Douglas A. Mackey.
    p. cm. (Clipper studies in the theatre, ISSN 0748-237X ; no. 10)
  "Synthesis of interviews conducted with Sydney H. Spayde over a period
of years."—Pref.
  Includes bibliographical references and index.
  ISBN 0-89370-316-8 (cloth). — ISBN 0-89370-416-4 (pbk.)
  1. Acting. 2. Movement (Acting). I. Mackey, Douglas A., 1947- . II.
Title. III. Series.
PN2061.S64 1993   93-9431
792'.028—dc20   CIP

FIRST EDITION

CONTENTS

Preface 5

Introduction...10

I. TRAINING..15
    You Are Your Instrument...............................17
    Finding Freedom on the Floor.......................18
    The Feet Can Speak......................................25
    A Space for the Voice....................................28
    The Rise and Fall of Emotion.......................30
    Breaking Through...33

II. AUDITIONING...39
    "No Acting Please!" 41
    The Unitive Art of Casting 43
    Seeing Through the Script...........................46
    "Saying" Something 50
    Cliché Movements and Line Readings.........53
    Loosening the Ears 58
    Positions and Oppositions 61

III. REHEARSING..65
    The Sense of Place 67
    Externalize While You Memorize...............68
    Creative Listening 71
    The Actor in the Grand Design 74
    The Third Dimension..................................78
    Taking Chances Safely...............................80
    Giving the Dialogue a Second Chance 82
    Platforms—Physical and Psychological.......85

"Aim for the End from the Beginning"....................88

Ongoingness 90

An Anatomy of Climax.......................................92

Incarnating the Character................................96

The Actorly Ego..97

Opening the Door 99

After the Fact 102

Doors into the Play 104

IV. PLAYING...109

Bridging Rehearsal and Performance 111

How Not to Have Fun 115

Playing Precipitatively....................................119

Of, By, and For the Audience............................120

Stage-Centered Plays.......................................126

Audience-Centered Plays 128

On Air 131

Entrances and Exits..134

Pro and Con...139

The Joy of Catharsis 141

What's Entertainment?......................................143

The Transcendent Quality of Acting.................145

Suggested Reading...151

Index..155

PREFACE

This book is the synthesis of interviews conducted with Sydney H. Spayde over a period of years. A veteran director of over 340 plays and founder of several theatres around the country, Syd speaks from a deep well of experience and from a passion for artistic quality.

I have attempted to distill the rambling brilliance of the interviews, and create not a textbook or a treatise, but rather an informal book of random knowledge. Though it follows a certain sequential logic, it can just as well be dipped into at any point for insight or inspiration.

The interest of this book, I believe, is that Syd's ideas about acting and theatre in general have the weight of authority behind them of a professional whose career has been unusually long, varied, and distinguished. He has remained vitally interested and involved in the theatre up to the present day.

Syd grew up in Rapid City, South Dakota, where he was exposed to a variety of artistic influences through his parents and aunt. From helping with props for the traveling stock companies that toured the Black Hills, he went on to the Northwestern University School of Speech, where he won national speaking contests and studied art, music, dance, and theatre.

After some professional work in Chicago, he became head of the theatre department at Yankton College, where one of his productions, Ibsen's *Peer Gynt,* brought him national acclaim and a graduate fellowship to the University of Iowa. There he studied theatre with E. C. Mabie, and art with Grant Wood.

After leaving Iowa, he spent the next twenty-five years as director or guest director in theatres throughout the country. He was associated with Kalamazoo Civic Theatre; Dock Street Theatre in Charleston, South Carolina; Grand Rapids Civic Theatre; Cain Park Theatre in Cleveland; and the Black Hills Playhouse. He taught and directed at Wayne State University and at Carnegie Tech (now Carnegie-Mellon). Many of his students went on to successful professional careers. Among them were William Ball, George Peppard, and Ellis Rabb.

In 1962 he became Professor of Theatre and Dean of Fine Arts at Parsons College in Fairfield, Iowa, where he staged a number of summer theatre festivals. These large scale productions featured established stars, such as Faye Emerson, Macdonald Carey, Basil Rathbone, Bob Newhart, and Pat O'Brien. At the final Parsons commencement exercise, Syd was honored with a Doctor of Fine Arts degree.

Despite his partial blindness and a number of eye operations, he continued to teach and direct after retirement, and on his 75th birthday, the theatre at Maharishi International University in Fairfield, Iowa, was renamed in his honor. He was selected by the National Endowment for the Arts as one of twenty handicapped artists in the United States to be featured in the book *Profiles in the Arts*. In 1988 he was awarded the first Art Cole Lifetime of Leadership Award from the American Association of Community Theatre. He and his wife Gladys now reside in Iowa City.

His former students do not forget him. He has earned their long-standing respect, admiration, and love. That speaks even more loudly than the list of his accomplishments, distinguished as it is.

This book began with input from many of his students over the years, who at Syd's request wrote up some of the most memorable "keys" which he had given them to help unlock their acting potential. The ideas and metaphors which recurred most often in their responses formed the basis of the series of interviews I conducted with Syd. I organized the material from the resulting transcripts into a manuscript which was then heavily revised by Syd and myself. Additionally, we would like to thank Jon Spayde and Nancy Harris for their editing and revisions, which added much to the clarity of the final product.

Syd professes to be more of a theatre practitioner than theorist, and the ideas which he expresses in these pages have all been tested through his many years of teaching and directing. They will mean the most to the reader who relates them to his or her own experience, either onstage or in the audience. Accordingly, the point of view in this book tends to fluctuate between that of the actor, the director, and the member of the audience.

As a teacher, Syd emphasizes the actor's physicality—visualizing, imagining, and coloring the character as much as possible before one actually speaks a line. For often what one does with the body tends to run counter to the memorized text that emerges from the talking head. Once the character is conceptualized and then taken inside, so that it informs the actor's physicality, the lines can emerge as if spontaneously. One of Syd's main ideas is that acting, which is based on one's experiences of observing people move, talk, and express emotion, is impeded by the written play text itself. The bookish script gets in the way, so that instead of a whole, believable representation of a human being, we have mainly a talking mouth, repeating memorized or written words, and ignoring the causes of the lines or words, causes which lie in the physicality of the character.

Good playwriting implies a lot about how characters stand, gesture, and move, beyond just the words they say. But because of the rather prevalent idea that the play is all in the words, the body starts moving self-consciously, rigidly, and mechanically, losing the flexibility,

7

rhythm, and variety it exhibits in everyday life. Also, consciousness of the script inhibits contact between the actors and promotes self-centeredness instead of an attitude of involvement with the audience and the other actors.

Syd talks about how a play is built on a structure of blockages or oppositions that must be felt in order for it to emerge as engrossing and exciting. Plays are about extraordinary people in the grip of unusual needs and problems. As articulate actors, we must fill ourselves with air from the diaphragm, which supports the sense of the extraordinary we are trying to project, and helps to make the oppositions vivid. The breathing is fundamental to good acting, as it supports the relaxation, vibrancy, resonance, richness, and warmth of the natural speaking voice. Syd teaches us to explore and extend line "readings," discovering the patterns of sound that the playwright heard.

During rehearsals, Syd encourages the actors to explore a play's abundant pro and con relationships. He has a strong sense for defining the currents of attraction and repulsion between characters. The sense of reality, he says, is heightened when a playwright sets up an expectation, then introduces its antithesis. Inexperienced players tend to reduce oppositions to near-absolute levels due to the ear's inurement in reading cadences. The play script is an abstraction of a living reality which must be transmitted to the audience in its full sensuous colors. Acting requires taking the playwright's imaginative structure and delivering it to the audience. As such, it involves creation, or rather re-creation, which is implicit in the word rehearsal, a re-hearing.

I was particularly fascinated by his concept of "breakthrough," of finding the key to believable acting. In this book he describes his own experience of breakthrough, which came when he was a student at

Northwestern, in the middle of a class in oral interpretation. He had a sudden realization that acting is just like being, except one is being in a role. At once it became easy for him to say the words of the script with a keen awareness of the playwright's intention. Syd believes that every good actor must, at some point, experience this.

To break through to a level where everything you do is intuitively right, you must learn to set aside the concentric ego, which is always worried about the effect of how one is coming across, rather than the cause motivating a speech or action. You can't attain this point through force of effort. But you can pave the way through work, dedication, concentration and an effort of intelligence. The actual moment of breakthrough often comes unexpectedly, in a flash, like a state of grace.

The following pages contain no certain formulas for realizing that ineffable peak experience. But they do represent the thoughtful and practical approach of a man who has spent his life helping others to find it.

Douglas A. Mackey
Fairfield, Iowa
August, 1993

INTRODUCTION

by Sydney H. Spayde

For the past few retirement years I have enjoyed keeping informed about the latest writings on experimental exercises, theories, methods, and alleged results with the acting arts. I wish such well-organized and vividly descriptive books had been available in the twenties when I was starting out. There were actually only about two or three then, and they didn't do much for me.

University theatres at that time, even the three or four best ones, were noted mainly for growing excellence in producing creative production work in scene design, costuming, lighting, sound, business, and propping. With acting and even directing they were generally ambivalent as to methods. Thus there was a good deal of criticism leveled against the university and college theatre by the professionals, basically to the effect that the students did not know how to act. It was said that if a young actor in New York wrote in his résumé that he was a college graduate, he rarely got a sympathetic audition. There was too much theory in college courses, and too little real, positive action in association with audiences of an average mix.

All that has changed notably. Academic theatre has improved, as has the level of acting instruction and criticism. I regard such books highly and have learned from them.

Many of the ideas contained herein have come my way through trial and error, as evidenced in actual productions, sensitively criticized. The directors of my generation attended that school or conservatory which had

proven success in a special area where we felt we needed expert guidance. This situation took added time and
money, which tended to render us "late bloomers" compared with today's young directors, who have benefited
from improved instruction in universities throughout
the country. We probably received some advantages,
though, through direct contacts with leaders in the subjects in which we sought expertise. It was the height of
excitement for me to learn the techniques of scene
painting from Jan Muncis, the director of the Art
Theatre, Riga, Latvia; Dalcroze Eurythmics from
Adolph Appia's grandson, and so on.

I believe there is one basic source from which you
learn, and that is the audience. As I have worked in
various areas of theatre production—community college, professional, arts festival—I have had no more single guiding theme in my work than that the audience,
by expressing its levels of approval in attendance,
applause, and continuing support, is the master teacher. Many books on the subject echo this theme, and I
wish to as well.

My interest in this book is not to expound a theory. I
am not an exponent of a particular method. I have
found people to be too marvelously idiosyncratic for
such approaches to be very helpful or valid.

What a few other authors stress, however, is something that I have been constantly impressed with—the
elements of acting that is within us every day. You may
take a day in your life and analyze the structure of
events therein. You are many different people in the
course of that day. You start out as one person, but
adapt and change according to circumstances—that is,
your job, the people you meet, the accidents that may
occur, the good times, the bad times—and you play
many different and amusing roles as you go. Moreover,
you do it with a certain amount of efficiency and color,
with various moral shadings, and with emotional vari-

eties summoned up from many sources of experience.

Yet so often, when we begin to make advances toward acting in a play, we seem not to be able to summon up the beliefs, experiences, and convictions which we really have with us almost all the time, the presence of which may have led to the casting for that role. Understanding ourselves, and in turn understanding ourselves in other characters whom we may be cast to play, is obviously the stuff of which acting is made. But when we are at first attracted to the theatre, we may likely have a series of preconceptions (some of which may be useful) as to how to read a play, try out for a play, and act on the stage. But there is a fair chance that these preconceptions are influenced by external observations of TV, movies, and local productions. Therefore we tend not to draw from *ourselves*. Through the years I have developed thoughts, ideas, attitudes, expressions, and metaphors that seem to have helped tyro actors discover how to tap that dramatic sense they already have and use in their daily lives.

An acting teacher soon runs out of formulas to use as explanatory tools. In one way or another, most of us have had to create our own personalized vocabulary when assisting an actor in translating the intentions of the playwright into full-minded and full-bodied stage presences. Acting is a very personal art depending on all parts of each person for its instrumentation. Because of the intimacy and complexity of the process, I found I had to originate my own analytical metaphors to describe it. I had to adjust my vocabulary to what I assumed to be the vocabulary of the person I was working with. If what I said still didn't help, then I changed my imagery, the syntax of my sentences, or the tonality of my voice in order to establish a confident, constructive rapport. It is not unlike what I imagine a psychiatrist does, only I don't think psychiatrists ever talk as much as directors frequently have to.

Apt and insightful metaphors are not easy to come by. They must set in action usable, meaningful images in the actor's mind which may have even motivated the playwright's original concepts behind the play's composition.

To find out which metaphors, words, phrases, and concepts had actually worked best over the years, I queried thirty students, educators, actors, directors, and designers who had studied with me. I asked them what metaphoric devices had the most lasting and consistent effect on successive acting roles, directing and designing projects. All of the ideas presented in this book were considered memorable and professionally dependable by a majority of those contacted.

To me, the test of these ideas has always been how they help the participants clarify their purpose, resources, and meaning. The process is one of the clearing away of non-essentials while advancing to the performance goal. We come to the "door" of the play's structure, which separates us from realization of that goal of entering the area wherein the playwright has chosen the most advantageous time, place, season, country, and social mores to convincingly express his ideas.

Taking the key which has been forged and fitted according to the playwright's formula, we may not only obtain entrance, but on entering may prosper in the newly created atmosphere and environment.

So with luck and a good deal of "play-work," the key fits; the door swings open graciously. We stand perhaps dazzled for a moment, and then we confidently survey, accept, and enter the revealed world of the play with joy and confidence.

This is one of the ideas and metaphors which have played well in my experimentations. Hopefully these may suggest other, more personal ways for the actor to enter and successfully inhabit the viable places of the playwright's work.

To Anna K. and Fred L., Estelle S. and Albert H.—
  who surrounded growing pains with music,
  dance, total trust, and good taste . . .

To Gladys C. and Jon F.—
  who endured and applauded at precisely the
  right times . . .

To Edward C. and Dina R., Hunton S., Grant W.—
  who challenged, criticized, and rewarded
  sparingly, constructively . . .

To Macdonald C., William B., Kenneth G.,Whitfield C.,
  George P., Hal H., Ellis R., Paul M.—
  who attended, questioned, enjoyed, and entered
  the performance place with me . . .

To Douglas M.—
  who listened, argued, judged, recorded, and
  edited with uncommon awareness and
  creativity . . .

To Basil R., Pat O'B., Margaret T., Faye E., Signa H.,
  Joe E. B., Dody G.—
  who taught us all while performing with top
  professional clarity and competence.

I

TRAINING

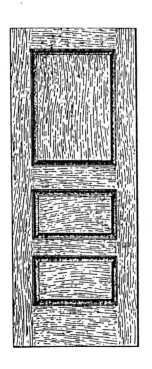

You Are Your Instrument

Anyone who works in the theatre for a period of time evolves a special interpretation of the work ethic. The "work" involved in playing refers to the time you spend to equip yourself for the task, and work for one is play for another. The tool you use, the instrument of your practice, is yourself, which makes that practice very intimate and animated. You don't have an inanimate instrument that you carry in a velvet lined box, which you can count on to perform in a predictable fashion if you don't let it get damp.

You are your instrument, and your body, mind, and spirit are fallible. For example, in all probability you were never intended to have a speaking mechanism at all: every part of the vocal instrument was primarily intended for functions other than vocalization, and is extremely prone to fatigue, as are the often overdeveloped muscles of the frame. Everything about the instrument, which has to be as finely tuned as any other kind of instrument, is dependent on proper health and digestion for its proper functioning. On top of that, the actor has to perform the dual function of being both the artist and the instrument at the same time.

Some people can view themselves as actor-technicians, completely separate from their instrument; others are unable to view themselves as detached from the operation of the body. This difference corresponds to an old controversy about training methods. Do you train like a technician from the outside in, or from the inside out? In either case, the actor, being an important technician of the theatre, faces a technical challenge—and must develop an apt and facile technique. On this score the actor trains largely according to his own balance of introversion and extroversion, the nature of his

17

physique, and his mental attitudes. An introspective type obviously needs to explore and work for explicitness. An extrovert needs to work for depth of understanding. There is always a delicate balance to be achieved and maintained, and I don't think any one method can work for everyone.

For introverts, method acting tends to be superfluous. Their problem is bringing their inner life to the surface, to externalize so we all may know and share whatever they want us to know. Often in their training it is hard work and little play for them to dance, to fence, and to develop stage deportment. That is not to say that they don't eventually enjoy these activities, especially when they feel they are rounding out their stage personalities.

For extroverts, delving into an authentic class working the fundamentals of the Method may be a helpful discipline in controlling random thoughts and movements. Organization of details affecting a complex character will be consecutive and meaningful instead of scattered. The technical approach intends to harness the external exuberance by internalizing the impulses that they may be controlled by more disciplined decisions. The rest of the company will appreciate knowing where and how you play the scenes, tomorrow night.

Finding Freedom on the Floor

I have often fancied that if we had, in prehistoric times, moved "on all fours," it would not be a bad idea to do the same when it came to playing out our rituals and celebrations. When the feet and legs are not caught up in the necessity of maintaining an erect position, they feel more mobile and sensitive, as they have a right to be. Most people overposition themselves on their feet, rigidifying their legs as a means of support, as if they were on a tipping boat that was threatening to upset them. They take a stance and set their feet on the floor as if in concrete. When they walk, you can hear the clumping of weight coming down. As a result, sensitivity and energy are unnecessarily lost.

You don't need to fear that when you feel more mobility and looseness in the ankles, knees, and thighs, your movement will become flighty and busy (although such a planned pattern of combined actions could be used for playing a bouncy comic character). There is a fleetness in the range of simple, normal movement, a firmly decisive "going to" and a "coming from." A rhythm pulses through the pleasures or sorrows of the scene, giving it ease of total body reaction and an ongoing quality. The rhythmic facility accounts for the measuring of time and distance on a stage, and makes effective entrances and exits possible.

This attunement of the body to the plotted action or situation needs to accompany the attunement of the voice and the mind. I have seen brilliant, articulate face, arms, and torso supported by a completely measured, rigidly detached pair of hips, knees, and ankles underneath it. I have seen bodies contradicting themselves, the upper half saying one thing, the lower half saying another. Hands will flutter, legs will stand stolid, while face and voice seem altogether disembodied. The effect is at times spastic, and it can be confusing, irritating, and misleading. In these cases, the total instrument has become disassociated from its parts. It has no unity.

When students begin to study duo scenes in acting class, they usually concentrate on speech patterns rather than confrontational action patterns (the "pros" and "cons"), and they are almost totally unaware of the space pattern (the "where"). They tend to stress mainly the immediately discernible "what" of the playwright's words with only token attention to the realities of the playwright's basic and fundamental "whys."

Everyone can speak. But can everyone project the scene designer's plan, the heat and cold of a space, the seasonal sensations, the day and night, and the psychology of place, time, and space, without dialogue? Here is where the creativity and the challenge come in: to vivify the author's and technical designer's choice of specific space and time; to position the body, mind, and spirit in the author's pattern of relationships; then to clarify further with the author's words.

Good acting arises from full physicality, the sensitivity that comes out of the fingertips and goes clear to the toes—especially to the toes, which are actually another set of fingers that happen to be burdened with the weight of the body and encased in shoes. In the training period I often like to get off the feet and give the leg muscles more of a chance to be expressive.

People have a great tendency to settle onto their heels when undecided about the motivations for their next move. But the moment the heels land, there is a "short-circuiting" of all the body energy—the "electricity." It goes right down through the heels and floor, where nobody needs it, down under the stage where there is no audience. Time and again I have found actors, having marched their pedestrian way through the play, responding to my suggestion: "Look, instead of marching to your own drum self-consciously through the scene, *waltz* through it, just to loosen the rigidity. Search for a different rhythm pattern, more related to full body action—both yours and the character's." Or simply: "Dance it!" This invariably helps. It directs the attention toward the potential freedom of the legs, ankles, and feet.

If the top and the bottom of the body are encouraged to reflect emotional flexibility, the middle will tend to take care of itself. The voice will tend to be centered in the body and will reflect the wonderful physical variations of positive and negative motivations, not to mention the full range in between, where probably most of the emotional keys to the play are available. The voice follows where the mind leads it.

Acting exercises may help keep the actor's mind in condition and his senses in synchronization. But such exercises are not necessarily a key to open the door to authentic performance. I have seen many people very proficient in theatre games and certain types of exercises, who immediately after successfully accomplishing them couldn't seem to apply the game experience to an acting project.

Responding to these cases, I have spent several years developing what I call floor exercises—which actually are, on experimental occasions, acting projects relegated toward playing "off the feet," hence on or toward the floor.

In floor exercises, we drop down on the floor and encourage the ankles to assume the pliability of wrists, and the feet to take on the responsibility of the hands for expressing feeling. The legs will soon seem to find a life of their own which contributes to the character's sensibilities. We say to our legs: "You have affirmative and negative sensual assignments. You help me a great deal if I allow my body full extension down there, to counter the top-heavy, mouth-centered tendency in acting." One breathes more openly on the floor as our awareness expands into a fullness of body sensuality.

Floor exercises counter the lower body insensitivity, which may exist from the neck down if hands and arms have not been encouraged during the growing-up years to practice and attain success in manual dexterity. Those who have not sawed, hammered, tilled, drawn, typed, or played ball have a tendency to move on stage in a curiously detached, fidgety way. The fingers will flick inside the palm of the hands. The feet will thud down in a monotonous two-beat rhythm. Most of this results from a lack of experience in total body control and/or confidence. It is an unconscious reflection of the tensions of a period of not having used the hands and legs in meaningful ways of communication.

When actors attend to the problem of entering a scene, their muscular tension may lead to a rigidity of mind and muscles, contributing to that ever-present state called stage fright, restricting their ability to fully portray the author's original intention of what they are required to feel and say. I try to have actors develop a scene from a relaxed position.. In floor exercises, they take any form or shape of prone positions, eliminating the strain on the legs and backs of thighs. It always strikes me as remarkable that this often helps them better to hear the author's intention as to the emotion and intelligence of the line, and not only to listen to but to "hear" the other actors as well, with that same sense of relaxed physical and mental awareness. This does not mean the actor will necessarily be playing the scene on the floor, but she will be playing it with a subtext or inner image based on an attentive relaxation.

Many times a character is required to play a transition from a state of tension to relaxation. I will ask the actor to gradually position the body on the floor, to roll and stretch. At these times, I encourage the actor to consciously begin to breathe easily and deeply. I also use the floor a good deal for developing diaphragm recognition, the better to relate breath control to the coloring of the voice in pitch, rate, force, quality, and the basing of a performing voice. Such exercises are continued until there is a feeling that the resonance is positioned well above and out of the throat.

Once on the floor, the actor may improvise all manner of stretchings and rollings, or partially lift onto elbows or knees, discovering bodily rhythms according to the feelings engendered by the lines she is speaking. It may take some actors awhile to discover this kind of fluidity or serpentine grace in their bodies. Many have simply not been aware that the body has an innate fluidity; that there is a flow of feeling from the fingers into the wrists and up the arms, and onward into the face and voice.

Once again we are encouraging a synchronization. Floor exercises help to bring a measure of organic flow into the body, by stretching, rolling, partially sitting; by feeling the freedom of the feet, legs, and ankles; by sometimes moving to the knee or to a sitting position and then flowing down out of it, while exploring a simple monologue, or even better, a favorite poem. We sometimes begin with abstract movement for its own sake, just letting go of all the muscles that are usually held rigidly for the sake of holding the body up; giving them a chance to play and kick unhampered as if they were swimming. Very soon an association between the character body, voice, intentions, and action begins to take over, to give the actor a fresh, creative approach which is free of the myriad clichés usually resorted to.

I have seen surprise light up an actor's face on the discovery, through floor exercises, of more imaginative, creative interaction of mind and body, of action and reaction, of the "self" of the character and the actor. I tell the actor then to move upright easily, being careful not to become rigid or clichéd in movement, and to maintain the looseness of the ankles, the muscles of the legs, and upper body. As long as she maintains this adjustment, she will continue to create the physical possibilities of the character.

Cliché movements and line readings are born of rigidities and tensions. If a young actor can be carried successfully in the direction of experimentation by starting on the floor, she can then be moved carefully to an upright position. No longer does the actor plant the heels or pound the floor—unless of course for a characterization point that has to be made.

The exercise gradually allows a person to stand and move with emotional logic, not merely for the sake of stage deportment. This means that a sensitivity and a selectivity are developed to the status of what is being presented on stage, the place, time, mode and movement replacing the mechanical impulse to move according to the traffic pattern by which the scene may have been blocked. How dispiriting it is when the director says, "Move to below right center," and the actor takes eight perfunctory steps without reason other than to get there.

During my callow youth, in directing my first fifty productions, I was often guilty of shuttling actors about the stage to get through an act in a limited period of rehearsals, figuring that later I would explain to them why they were there. Sometimes I did, and sometimes the actors discovered the reasons for themselves. Certainly I have designed the movement with a motive in mind. I do not send actors to the side simply to get them out of the way, but because there is a negative pulse that takes them away from the action. I note and feel little elements of negativity in the nature of the actor's walk, perhaps a hesitancy in the step or resentment in the head and neck, a pulsing of some of the muscles that projects the disappointment that took him out of the scene. I suggest the actor find the line in the play as just a further explication of what the body has been telling us.

If a line flows obviously from the physical action, the voice and the body will present a fine parallel. Floor exercises assist in discovering and developing that kind of unity of being and feeling. There is true excitement in the stage life of the young actor when he learns that the body is entirely capable of explicit communication, which is, more often than one imagines, the true source for the spoken word.

The Feet Can Speak

We tend to become slightly self-conscious, or even worse unconcerned, when and if we face the necessity of locomotion on the stage, probably because our feet are at a variable distance underneath us in everyday life. Our eyes are some five or six feet above our feet, and we are generally in more frequent and intimate contact with events at eye level. So long as our shoes are comfortable, we do not think of our feet or have an emotional connection to them, except perhaps for an ingrown toenail or a tenacious corn.

When I have a relaxed group of actors on stage before rehearsal, it is informing to watch the variety and vitality of their body messages, especially the informal revelations of their footwork. Then when early rehearsal begins, suddenly the feet become formal, as if they are in a TV ad for shoes and socks.

Feet have marvelous rhythms, reflecting and emphasizing even the subtle upper body messages of torso, arms, and hands. They say a lot if they are encouraged. We are so speech-conscious, so memorization-conscious, we tend to assume that no part of our body other than our mouth has anything much to say. We may tend to disembody ourselves. We cut off the bottom half of our body, which is worth a lot when we consider that the stage is usually elevated and the audience sees us on stage from quite a different, full-figured angle. This is particularly true when upper levels and platforms are part of the set, bringing the total body image even more emphatically to the audience awareness.

An actor who has realized the potentialities of sensitive, creative footwork is exciting to watch. Such an actor allows the thought to permeate downwards, through the body, the legs, and into the feet, then to observe and listen for what they may be able to say on behalf of his character and situation of the moment. A number of times, when I have had a vertical curtain I could lower from the top, I have had my actors play a scene aware that only the lower half of the body would show. When they realized their upper halves were not going to be available to the audience, they found they could suggest many facets of the basic character and situation: shuffling with confusion and illness, springing with tingling young impatience, stumbling with inhibiting fear, striding with bashful passion. Even their voices changed—lowered and leveled—and there was much more care, precision, and sensitivity engendered by the synchronization of all body units capable of communication to an audience.

In expressing age, the feet are much more convincing than that old cliché of many actors, the pinched voice. There are many old people whose voices never crack. Young people tend to play older roles with both the voice cliché and a halting rheumatic shuffle—the latter especially for grandfather. The simple fact of age has to be supported with the evidence of the emotional attitudes that develop over years of human life. The physicality must be carefully observed, selected, practiced, and played in support of the playwright's directions.

Occupational types can be well characterized through physicality alone. You can project a doctor, lawyer, professor, steelworker, or laborer without uttering a word. When you briefly take the mouth out of dominance, young actors will be challenged and enjoy making the rest of their body perform.

The most impressive use of the legs and feet I ever saw occurred many years ago in a production of Deval's play *Tovarich*. Marta Abba, an Italian actress at that time called one of the world's greatest, had come to the

United States. She was a close friend of Pirandello, who also wrote plays for her. Her entrances and exits were exhilarating. I had never seen an actress move with such controlled high energy, alacrity, and buoyancy. When she moved up a flight of stairs, it was as if she actually left an afterimage. It was hard to believe.

Several years later, when I was directing in Cleveland at The Cain Park Theatre, it turned out that Ms. Abba lived only a few blocks from the theatre. When she decided to return to the stage, it fell to me to direct her production of Pirandello's *Right You Are If You Think You Are,* a play written for her years before. Her original role was that of a fascinating young woman, but for this production she chose to play Signora Frola, an equally fascinating 80-year-old. Ms. Abba made it a condition of her participation that we should have five-hour rehearsals. We had been used to three hours, at the most four. Furthermore, she never liked us to sit down, and she herself did not rest in five hours. Over and over she repeated: "You will lose your tension, your interest, your vitality, if you sit down."

We have long known that in stage movement you must probably double the energy you project when you sit down because your visual image has dwindled by half. If you don't know this, it is quite possible to fade out of the picture, for this and other associated reasons. To me Marta Abba's dominating stage presence, even when sitting, was epitomized in the power of her legs, which were beautifully shaped, but strong as steel cords. She had a muscular development that even bicyclists rarely have. And she was always exhorting the rest of us to get up on our toes and strengthen our legs.

She had an almost extrasensory awareness of the energies of the other actors—when, where, and how they were being expended. There were several ensemble scenes, and though she would be downstage, she would suddenly stop, point to the back, and say, "There are two people back there who are not in the scene." She could sense that their energy was not in sync with what was planned to happen on stage. As she brought the rather awesome awareness of her talent and experience—and her conditioned legs—to the actors in rehearsal, she created a memorable affirmation of the power of moving the acting body over the stage spaces with superior physical resources.

A Space for the Voice

Some of us can't run as fast as others because we haven't practiced running. Likewise, some people are less expressive than others because they haven't practiced the effects their voice is capable of. I listen to the monotone of coaches on TV exhorting their teams. I'm told that a monotone can either put a person to sleep or drive him mad. So perhaps by inflecting in different ways, we are preserving both our waking awareness and our sanity.

I try to show people how to evolve intelligent action and vocal awareness at the same time. Since we are aware of how these elements are coordinated in everyday life, we are not imposing on the acting technique something that no one knows anything about. When we have an extraordinary day, our bodily responses are filled with color, vibrancy and tensions. Often on stage, responses seem inhibited, controlled, dull, and monotonous.

I want my actors to feel that the space they occupy is itself dramatic. On a beautiful back porch, with a lovely grove of trees, backed by sun and clouds or moon and stars, one can look out and watch the light change during the morning, afternoon, and night, reacting to the subtle changes of color and mood in the course of the seasons. Such a space is full of emotional power that the playwright can and does use. His choice of space and place is presumably made to best enhance the essence of his story, and the times of day are chosen to advance the plot physically and psychologically.

As an actor moves into the playwright's world, he must be sensitive whether he is playing in outdoor or indoor spaces. The voice should reflect whether he is in a closed room or on a mountain top. Its emotional ranges must parallel external spaces and events—such as great storms, with wind howling, lightning flashing, and seas raging. Shakespeare suggested a lot of heavy weather by the power of speech alone, as from *King Lear:* "Blow, winds, and crack your cheeks! Rage! Blow!"

The enemy to vocal effectiveness, and to other types of theatrical effectiveness, is being too cautious, self-conscious, and self-contained. One should have a willingness to take chances and open oneself to the essence of all the scenes and the intentions of the other people in the play space.

The traditional elements of vocal variety—pitch, rate, force, and quality—may be invoked occasionally to help save us from monotones or tiresome overstressing of line after line. Over the last few million years, we have managed well the use of our vocal cords, which were little muscles designed to keep masticated food from going down into the lungs. We've managed to make our gentle little wordlike sounds articulate, using our lips, teeth, and tongue, which were designed for mastication. We have given air support with the diaphragm, which was used to help the lungs oxygenate, thereby gaining a reasonable amount of volume, and by a bit of control added some resonance. Everything we use for speech was designed primarily for other body functions.

Even so, we have learned to be very expressive. We double and triple the exactness of a pretty clumsy instrument by our experimentation with pitch, rate, force, and quality. We do this always by appealing to the ears. We ask them to listen, that we may be informed, that we may perceive the facts that we need for action. Receiving this information, we file it away for future use and possible action. We *hear* and remember.

To listen is to perceive; to hear is to learn. All of this fundamental function in initiated by the mind deciding to articulate an opinion or a conviction which is turned over to the voice-box to enunciate for all concerned, who by listening may be inclined to learn and in turn take desired action.

The Rise and Fall of Emotion

"I am not anti-method, but on the stage I have to know what I am going to do every minute. For that you need technique; you can't improvise a performance every night. By the time a play is ready to open, I am so immersed in the character I am playing that I can be confident the lines will come, because they are the lines that the character would speak in that situation. But the framework of the performance has to be set; it can't depend on the way the actor feels that night. Actors who become so absorbed in self-analysis that they disregard the other actors—or, worse yet, the play itself—are misusing the Method; they are using it as an argument to justify their own self-indulgence. That is inexcusable. The actor is there only to deliver the play the author has written. That is his only reason for being."

— Jason Robards, Jr., quoted in *Theatre Arts*

On occasion an empathic actor feels his part so deeply, he doesn't seem to seek for a certain kind of help from his audience, whom he apparently considers an intruder on his privacy. That actor often proclaims that now he's *really* acting. And that's usually when he's pretty bad, when what he produces looks and sounds like acting. If the characterization hasn't transcended the technique to produce whatever it was intended to be—a romantic, or melodramatic, or tragic, or comic moment—if the mechanics show, then it's not enjoyable or probably intelligible for the other actors and therefore for the audience.

I think I have obtained my results generally without a Method approach, although any actor with a good mind and body is going to carry elements of "reflective recall" to his or her rendezvous with the dramatic moment. If you had to play a scene around a character who was dying, how could you exclude your own experiences of death from what you were feeling?

In cases of high emotional pitch, of jealousy, fright, or anger, for example, young actors are rather inclined not to feel the rhythms which produced the vibrancy of that moment. Some characters are slow to anger and others quick, and the awareness of these variations should be integral to their portrayal, based, of course, on the playwright's plan for the characters involved in the moment. Even more important is the release from the emotional peak, and the aftermath of the emotion, which unfortunately tends to last only about fifteen seconds for many actors and perhaps for some playwrights. The director and actors must be prepared on occasion to exercise their taste, experience, and judgment in creating a more believable response.

In real life, an outburst of emotion almost always takes as long or longer to recede than it does to advance. Once that adrenaline has been pumped into the body, it raises the temperature and the breath rate to cause the arms, ears, and knees to respond for quite a while afterward. Many actors do not really appreciate this rise and fall vividly enough. Sometimes the "fall" requires the extension of business after an emotional moment, the motivating of long pauses, not only for their own sake, but for creative recession from the vibrancy of the moment. By interaction with the other actors, one should pass through a process of "cooling down" to the level for which the playwright has written the next sequence.

Use no more energy than is necessary to make the moment believable. Energy is a colorful component of all levels of intention and interpretation. Normally we have no trouble with it in our everyday life because it is naturally in proportion. When we enter into other lives, those of our characters, it may not be proportionate and may have a tendency to be overplayed too insensitively for empathic belief.

In some non-professional theatre productions, the apparently weak moments are those that involve peaks of emotion. The actors don't quite know how to peak, or at what level a particular height of emotion is logically best to be played. When you judge the full pattern, the ebb and flow of the heightened scenes, you can easily tell whether the energy is too high and too soon, when little is left to "top" the succeeding scenes. Otherwise, when the climax is due to fall, it never arrives, having been rendered anticlimactic by earlier extravagances.

I would like you to be highly sensitive and aware of the playwright's intentions and techniques in achieving the cyclical rhythms of emotional actions and reactions. Again, use only enough of the apparent emotional energy to create the truest reality that you know and feel—no more and no less.

Breaking Through

"Where the actors of the Moscow Art Theatre were 'naturalistic,' Duse was nature. There was nothing between her and truth; she was truth. She has mastered the craft of acting so completely that she no longer needed to use it consciously. There was no hiatus between the thoughts and feelings of the characters she played, and herself as their interpreter. It was one process. In most actors this process is divided; first there is awareness of the thought, then the technical means used to convey it."

— Eva Le Gallienne, in *The Mystic in the Theatre: Eleonora Duse*

I use the word "breakthrough" to describe that moment at which insight descends and acting becomes being. For the actors I have trained over the years, the term seems to have meant something. Probably everybody who has experienced it has done so under a different set of circumstances. It is rather mysterious. The knowledge of it, once gained, is never lost. It is subject to practice, as any technique is, and I have seen cases where it phases in and out. But generally, when you get it, you have it.

A breakthrough may be a sudden realization of what the playwright and director meant when they were saying that a given moment has the believability of life. Certainly, up to this point, you've wanted your contributions to be judged as good acting, and if they weren't quite that, it may be because you had not quite taken into yourself the facts of the scene. Perhaps the interpretation was a little superficial, the lines recited or cadenced rather than spoken or said. Perhaps the body was too "stately." Perhaps the scene had a feeling of having been rehearsed rather than performed.

But you can aim to transcend these contrivances and go on into the spontaneity implicit in the scene, breaking through to an "illusion of the first time." At that moment, a person's awareness seems to crack open, a light comes forth, and he says, "Of course, this is what I meant!" There is a new tone uncovered in the voice, and in the body and spirit a feeling of emancipation.

Once I was directing Shaw's *Candida* in Detroit's first arena performance, and the young actor who was playing Marchbanks was having some problems. He was an Italian who spoke quite explicitly and expertly, illustrating every line, almost as if he were doing National Theatre for the Deaf. One rehearsal night he let me tie his hands behind him. We did not anticipate the consequences—for several seconds he could not make a sound. He had to rethink his whole mind-body connection. Finally, after taking a few deep breaths, he broke the tension and spoke. To the joy of everybody there, he was suddenly speaking from a new attitude. The experience was for him a literal breakthrough. From then on the play soared, and it was a great success.

The breakthrough is a highly individual experience, and you don't know when or how it's going to take place. It happened for me in the School of Speech at Northwestern University during private lessons in literary interpretation. My teacher, Miss Hazel Easton, was sweet and patient, and I had an immediate rapport with her. I was not the slowest, but far from the quickest in achieving the breakthrough.

I do not know why, on a particular afternoon at 2:30, it suddenly worked. I do know that for the first time I was not standing up in front of Miss Easton showing her that I had studied my lessons. Knowing full well that I had studied them, I felt that I was taking my own time, and with my own sense of what was exciting, beautiful, mysterious, and frightening about my material. I was performing it to her as if the playwright's words were my own now. I was out of the cadenced rhythms which had been imbedded in my ears and mind from the composite sounds I had learned from listening to actors, politicians, ministers, professors, and radio announcers.

And yet, immediately after finishing, I didn't think I had done very well. Miss Easton just sat and smiled. Then, after letting me cool off a bit, she told me, "All right. It has happened. You never will forget this." I said, "But I'm just saying it, I'm not acting it." She said, "Yes, that's what it's all about."

I remember thinking, "How stupid I've been all this time!" I had been in a shell of recitation, and although I had been in many plays up to that point, no director had been able to show me how to create my speech and physicality out of the situations, using the words and motives supplied by the playwright. It was a delirious moment. I started hearing things other actors were saying in such a fashion that I could answer in a saying mode rather than a reciting mode. And I never got back into any manner of false, stiff, unconvincing delivery again.

Hardly a month goes by when this doesn't happen to one of my students. There is a series of steps I can take them through to attempt to achieve a breakthrough, but I don't know any two students I've ever taken through the same steps. Initially, I just talk to them. Our conversation generally shapes in their ears their own voice, their own speech rhythms, and helps them become aware of the underlying process of finding the words, phrases, and emotion to make a point clear to me. Often I establish eye contact with them, then see if they can, without breaking it, make emotional contact with some of the material they've been studying.

The actor needs a sense of controlling his material rather than being controlled by it. When he recites, the material is controlling him. By definition, to "recite" is to speak words from memory. Recitation is metric. We try to get in a certain number of words while a mental metronome is ticking. When we really say something, it is rhythmical; we pause, for example, when we want to search for words or thoughts. Often an actor will read perfectly: breaking, pausing, accenting, and developing the pitch, rate, force, and quality of the playwright's words and intended inflections, only to lose the whole feeling for the words when he memorizes. The monotony takes over. Many times I use theatre games to emphasize this. Greet a friend on the street whom you haven't seen in five years; then greet him as if you had memorized the speech. In real life, he would probably look at you as if you had lost your mind.

Often the breakthrough happens in private lessons and/or rehearsals rather than in an actual full-scale rehearsal. On the other hand, I have had students who were unable to reach that level of believability in private go into a play, surrounded by others who have no problem with it, and find themselves spontaneously giving back what they are offered.

When an actor breaks through during a rehearsal, I love to go up to him and say, "That's it." It usually surprises everybody, and what is best about it is that it's so good for the other actors who are around. They may have been playing at a near-breakthrough level for some time, and the mood or aura of one of their group breaking through gives them the impetus to take that little final step past the rigidities of the moment into creative release. They become overjoyed and start smiling. It's like a cool shower, a new physical sensation, almost a rebirth. And the rest of the rehearsals will very nearly take care of themselves. In recent years this desirable situation has been described in such terms as "taking chances safely"—the safety net underneath having been placed by intelligent blocking.

Actors on occasion come to a near-breakthrough, then on the next night aren't close to it at all. This sort of experience is not necessarily the actor's fault. There may be other factors he is having to cope with in the scene, such as actions and reactions from other actors that are not intelligent or true enough. However, when a breakthrough occurs, it is infectious, and an actor fresh in that feeling naturally spreads it to others.

The breakthrough needs to occur at a fairly primary stage in an actor's training. Until and unless the actor clearly perceives the rhythms and cadences of natural speech in both himself and the character he is presenting, he cannot move on to believably play a variety of character types. And he must greatly enjoy his playing in the physical sense. When he is in a state of mind that is not only comfortable but exhilarated, he listens and hears well. He catches the notes that the playwright intended.

II

AUDITIONING

"No Acting Please!"

The audition is a touchy time for actors. It is a perfectly natural occasion for the presence and display of nervousness. The confidence of the director has to be dominant; it is up to him to establish a warm, pleasant rapport at the earliest point, even as people are coming in the door. In the professional theatre there are some who do this and others who do not. A professional actor will be able to understand and likely withstand any buffeting that may occur. But in the amateur theatre the director should be careful to be constructive from the outset. (By the way, I use the word "amateur" with due admiration, for it defines an activity enjoyed by almost any group, mainly for recreational values and awards. Here the word is used to describe a person who cares for and loves what he does. There are professional actors who would do well to revert to the amateur attitude once in a while.)

From the beginning, I like to be immediately available, meeting or shaking hands, perhaps supplying informational paperwork, answering questions, and if possible establishing rapport. In a few minutes of casual contact, I may learn as much about an unfamiliar actor as I do hearing him or her read under a more stressed situation. For a first audition, I'm usually satisfied to have the actors sit in a circle of chairs on stage, perhaps rising once in a while later to meet an actor across from them. I'm interested in the quality of the voice, its energy, its placement, and its uniqueness. I encourage the actors not to cover up their individuality with trying to overlay with a finished performance. It doesn't hurt for them to know the play in advance, as long as they don't try to produce it for this audition. Thus, I never use the word "acting" in an audition.

Instead, I always ask the actors to "present" or "explore" a scene.

Certainly in auditions, I want my potential acting talent to be informed of the play, its background, and its particular style and treatment; this allows them to be comfortable with the event and with me as director. I try to make it apparent that the evolvement of the play is going to seem, at its best, to occur with "the illusion of the first time." And since this is very much the actual first time, there may occur some truly fresh and authentic saying of the lines. Listen attentively!

I am as much interested in people interacting as I am in acting. Sometimes I have to put a hold on people because they are so anxious to *act,* to get up there and declaim phrases regardless of whether or not it is a declamatory speech. They will try out for a Wilde play with a brittle, rushed assumed wittiness not even Oscar could have achieved. People seem so anxious to provide all the affectations you don't want, that I consider myself successful in the audition if I've managed to create, in a spirit of good fellowship, a kind of negativity. Let's not have all this glibness, this recitation, this cadenced speech, I suggest. Let's not sound so unbelievably eager, fresh, and on top of things. This covers up the relaxed voice and body, the seeing eye and the hearing ear I need to discern that they may possess and can therefore impart to an important character.

Actors are often not aware of the color and nature of their personalities in the same way that the director or other people may be. One of the charming foibles of people interested in theatre is that they want to come on and be someone entirely different from themselves. To them their success lies in not being recognized by their neighbors: "You were so good, we didn't know you!" This is a pleasant idea, and it may be an achievement of sorts.

On the other hand, when you see an artist perform,

you expect to enjoy and value his characteristic stamp. You don't find the great painters painting like somebody else. You know a Van Gogh when you see a Van Gogh. You enjoy being aware of musicians' unique authority by the tonality, superior technique, and the particular magnetism of their personality as a composer or performer. The same may be said of dramatists and designers of scenes, lighting, and costumes. There is only one "you," and that "you" is to be recognized, respected, enhanced, and presented in the company of other disciplined talents. As a creative and experienced director, you want to respond to every bit of individuality that the aspirant possesses.

The Unitive Art of Casting

Actors at the point of auditioning should be aware that the director wants to arrive at a comfortable solution of the casting problem. The director wants to do as little work or readjustment as possible, and tries to develop an almost extrasensory awareness as to whether or not the chosen actor will be sympathetic with the character which is to be played. This does not necessarily mean that the actor is like the character; on the contrary, often it is a matter of choosing somebody to a degree dissimilar enough that he or she can be objective about the character's habits and beliefs.

I once directed *The Women* by Claire Boothe Luce, in which there is the role of a very charming, witty, and catty villainess. I had a lady with a sort of "meow" sound in her voice and a sinuous grace of the body, so I cast her for the part. But it didn't work well, for as it turned out in this community she *was* considered a rather catty lady. This double dose of feline ferocity unbalanced the rather obvious plot. I later discussed this problem with a more experienced director, who told me that in this case it would be better to cast the most personable and cool lady you could find who had the requisite feline bodily attributes, because she would be the most highly sensitive to the subtle machinations of the character. I learned this principle early, and it is true.

One obvious means of selection is by age and physique. Actors with a more mature presence will probably be selected to play the "character" or eccentric roles, whereas those with less mature body and facial characteristics will probably explore the younger or "juvenile" roles.

Certainly it is helpful to have a sprinkling of previously successful experience in the cast, mainly to help create rapport and sympathetic relationships. A play, and every aspect of it, is an intimate experience. In many cases of insufficient rehearsal time, this intimacy is arrived at out of desperation, close to the end. One can only conjecture that if it had been sought for and realized from the beginning, the play would have been five or six times more cohesive. For that reason, I never hesitate to conduct enough callbacks to convince myself that we have assembled a caring and congenial group, even if rehearsal time is short. Better to get the most earnest and interacting ensemble with the right chemistry that you can from the start, rather than get excited, choose too quickly, and have to work out the problems later. This becomes of total importance with popular family plays.

When I know the pluses and minuses of the actors and the script, it becomes my job to meld them together, and put the strong people where they will lend strength—not necessarily in the strongest plot roles. Often the strongest part is so well-written that a person who is adequate will develop the necessary strength while rehearsing and playing. But in the weaker sections of the play, where it could fall apart, the stronger actors may be needed more sorely and may well learn additional techniques to last out a career.

All performance artists have a fundamental need to freshen their techniques by accompanying other artists; in other words, playing into the emotions, interpretations, rhythms, and beats, supporting all the many tints and shades of the performer, not only assisting but enlarging the indicated intentions. In repertory company training, the major role of last night supports the major tonight, who was the minor of last night.

Recently on Public Radio, Mr. David Amram, following a dual improvisation with Marian McPartland, another famous jazz pianist, was most articulate, not only on the values obtained by the close emotional union of the performing personalities, but also on the need for the performing ego to be as disciplined in a supporting status as when playing the lead role. The composer may write exceptionally subtle nuances into the accompanying, supporting material which often demands just as brilliant technique as do the dominant moments. Mr. Amram commented further on the modern dissonances common to almost all forms in which an opposition has to be achieved at times out of key and rhythm. He felt these are enhanced more positively by accompaniment than by dominant performance. The more sensitive and proficient the support, the more exciting and successful the presentation. Ms. McPartland added that accompanying or supporting each other's interpretations therefore strengthens the individual performances.

Ultimately what makes a superior acting ensemble is when the supporting roles are played by fine, experienced actors who contribute subtle and energizing accompaniments to the main actors. We want to be able to distribute the various types of talents and weaknesses in the best constructive positions.

When I finally cast them, I will know pretty well

how and at what rate each actor will be able to grow. Ultimately it depends on what the playwright wanted to say to the audience, and what sort of mechanics and personality colors he set up to do it. Having determined this, the director and actors try to move in the same direction, toward the realization of the situations set up by the playwright. We strive for unity, clarity of intent, directness, simplicity, impact, emotional truth and color.

Seeing Through the Script

"It's a very bitter pill for the actor to swallow, to be told that the other person is more important than you are, but you have to believe this. It must become your religion."
—Sanford Meisner, quoted in
The New York Times

Auditions always create different levels of nervousness, and nervousness is not helped by creating a formal atmosphere. What is needed is a friendly businesslike arrangement of assistants and necessary equipment. Under most circumstances, the atmosphere can well be arranged to have a less formal "performance" atmosphere, in favor of a more warm, experimental searching for the best resources. You are looking for an actor who can clarify natural problems. That is not the same as one who may read well on sight—often this actor is producing a kind of glib monologue that rarely gains much depth or dimension. I have had excellent actors who have dyslexia and really can't read easily, but they possess understanding and can indicate the presence of the other actors.

The script, in the form of the physical book, is a necessary evil. It's a little thing of paper and black print all neatly punctuated, sentenced and paragraphed, made to be eventually stored on shelves. It's the deadest and most inert of all the aspects of the theatrical process, but it happens to be the one that is first put in direct contact with the most alert part of it, the actor's mind and body. Unfortunately, too often the inert triumphs over the alert.

I suspect this goes back to reading, which is absolutely necessary; that is, the eye has to be cast on the page and a concept of the words has to be formed. But what do we do in reading aloud? We tend to monotonize the voice, ignore our surroundings, and allow the body to rigidify. The arms holding the book set the shoulders up as a tight instrument, and if a person is standing, he assumes a heel-in-the-ground, stonelike stance. Right away the life that is inherent in the script, the logical, believable, colorful, conversational intentions of the playwright, are suppressed, muddled, and confused.

How can personal warmth triumph over the coldness of the book? It makes an observable difference if a person holds the book informally in one hand. Holding it in two hands sets up a wall; it insinuates vertically, forming a psychological and even an actual barrier between the actor and other actors, and between the actor and the eventual audience. Instead, handle the book almost like a property, not always keeping it rigidly available to the eyes. This position may occasion a series of slight pauses—so what? Playwrights write with as much sensitivity to the pauses inherent in the spoken line as to the words. Aim to give an easy rhythmic flow rather than a metric beat to the line.

If a person, from overeagerness or a lack of experience, does not bring a generous part of himself to the first readings of the script, he may tend to read himself out of the part. He has little chance at really getting underneath the words or finding the warmth, humanity, and believability of the character. I converse with the actors before and after a reading. And many times I can cast far more accurately from an interesting conversation than I can from a reading, if that reading has been overworked, unhearing, egocentric, and overstressed—simply expressed, dealing with the "what" and not the fundamental "why."

When an actor has to read a letter on stage, how does he convince the audience that he's reading, when in reality he has memorized the text? He often turns it into a monotone and he speaks rather more to himself, or may scan it rapidly, as if to prove his facility. We know what reading cadences sound like, and unfortunately that same lack of vocal selectivity and variety is evident at many auditions.

One hopes that the actor is sensitive to saying words and phrases, and not just reading sentences factually. The ear is the essential instrument by which one can tell the difference. But many actors are not fully aware that as they are speaking the words, everyone is hearing them, thereby raising questions as to the depth of believability. The tyro actors' ears are merely registering the fact that they've finished a sentence; memorization has been accomplished and delivered; now it's time to start a new sentence. They may be glued psychologically to that inanimate entity, the script, perhaps due to shyness, nervousness, or simply by previous reading habits.

It requires very little coaching or directing to say to a person, even on a first reading, "Handle your script so easily that you can establish both eye and ear contact with the other persons." This encourages a more relaxed attitude and relationship. I advise the young actors, "Instead of gluing yourself to the book and occasionally glancing up at the other actors, reverse the process: fasten your attention on them and occasionally glance at the book for self-prompting." The ability to scan quickly varies from person to person, but if you can get an actor to scan a phrase or two and then adjust it to the other actors' needs and positions in the scene, then he will be basing his reading on the lively interplay inherent in the soul of the script.

Most of us know by experience that when we become an object viewed at a distance, on a stage or platform, we are viewed quite differently than when we walk into a room or sit down for dinner. Our physical language changes accordingly. People are often not aware that whether they want it or not, their body message is projecting across to people who are viewing them. In a relaxed audition, where the director and other participants are kept at a distance which the auditioner can accept as the audience's space, and where the actors can be encouraged to take a good look at each other, they will have an easier time "loosening up" their physical language. With the body free to move impulsively, even creatively, it doesn't take long for a person to use the script not as an obstacle but as a necessary and pleasant resource.

I emphasize the fact that the center of attention is beyond the book, where the lines and cues have necessarily been recorded. The actor who is a very explicit, beautiful reader, but who shyly glances up at another person, and in doing so doesn't see him, isn't any ideal. When new people are surrounded by an attitude of relative ease in those around them, and can feel that they are being accepted, looked at, and listened to, they are reminded of the human factors involved in the play. Then the audition becomes a warm experience and not a styled, rigid exercise in reading.

As actors we always depend upon the other people in a scene; the way we hear them determines how we will respond. The director takes for granted that the actor trying out knows how to read the English language. An audition is not a reading; it is, literally, a "hearing." A rehearsal is a "re-hearing." The ability to listen accurately, creatively, sensitively and respond from that basis should be cultivated from the very beginning of the production process, the audition.

"Saying" Something

In the course of a day, listen to the normal conversations in the shop, on the street, in the classroom, club meeting, and at home. The range of inflections is wide and the varying pitch, rate, force, and quality is revealing of changing subjects, moods, pros and cons.

But when we take up a script, assume another character's vocabulary and syntax, attitudes, moods, and step on stage, the variety of vocal range, pitch, force, and quality tends to shift toward an unconvincing, uneasy monotone and monorhythm. The vocal equipment is inclined to constrict toward the upper ranges, while the arm and shoulder muscles tighten. It is uncomfortable for actors and audience alike.

There is a type of performance pitch very common among radio and television announcers, particularly sportscasters. It is my unproven theory that people who listen to a lot of this telegraphic sort of delivery absorb by a type of auditory osmosis, the bombardment of vocal patterns spoken loudly without much regard to making sensitive sense. The same is true of many car, beer, and political commercials, with their trite triads of pitch and misplaced emphasis and elevated pitch which nevertheless gets recorded in our mind's ear, even when we try to reject it consciously.

Often in auditions, when I find a person's voice tending to ascend to the top of its range, I take time to explore the full extent of the natural, comfortable, median range, from top to bottom. If a piano is handy, I use it to give an awareness that between the possible highest and lowest notes of the speaking voice there is a comfortable range, down usually some three to five notes from the top high and up three or four from the low bottom. The actor has probably been using this median range all day long, and even if something exciting has happened, the voice has probably not reached the "reading" pitch, which invariably is up several shrill notes from the norm.

So I say: speak comfortably from inside yourself. We know for a fact that when eye contact is established with another personality, the voice will tend to lower in more or less direct psychological and physiological adjustment. When we greet an old friend, for example, we do not generally ascend in our vocal range to talk to him unless we're under positive or negative stress. The eye contact and person-to-person feeling allow the voice to settle into a meaningful expressive range.

Anything that can be said or devised to lessen the actor's (not the character's) personal tension will be helpful, for almost all stress elements tend to raise the voice toward an unnatural level of departure for playing a pliable and sensitive range of emotions. This is a matter of physiology: that when the vocal cords tighten, the pitch heightens tonally as well. There are too many play productions, especially on opening nights, which are pitched about a musical third above the optimum range. Thus an over-stressed quality may come across the footlights that is not intended in the purpose and style of the play. It sends a message into the audience: "I'm personally nervous, I'm tight and tense, I'm not enjoying, I'm not performing, I'm still rehearsing"—even during the most relaxed scene in a relaxing play. There are, of course, moments that are intentionally stressed, but that is a very different matter. The playwright and actor choose to creatively stress them, and the stress is communicated to the audience via their combined, coordinated techniques. The effect is to reveal the state of the character, not the actor.

Sometimes I almost simplistically tell people to

"say" their lines, especially in the early process of rehearsal, and to keep the full implications of that verb in mind. In my days at the Northwestern University School of Speech, we theatre majors were all trained in the art of literary interpretation. Edith Sitwell once came to the campus. On the poster, underneath her portrait in a compact composition showing her in full profile with her famous brothers, thus featuring their uniquely shaped noses, I was delighted and astonished to see the words: "Dame Edith Sitwell will *say* a program of her poetry." How utterly correct the phrase was! She came out to a musical entrance, with wild flaming hair, a heavily made-up face, and wearing a medieval gown of vivid green and gold brocade. Then out of this scintillating, dazzling creature came as controlled and conversationally poised a voice as you could ever hear. While there were complicated and involuted images and rhyme schemes, double and triple rhythms, points and counterpoints, she *said* her complicated poems, what a powerful and simple experience it was to listen to her, to understand emotionally and empathically every moment of every poem. Her "saying" was in contrast to the common tendencies toward intoning, with imposed flourishes and intoned intervals, as in the case of Henry Stephenson, Chicago's favorite local poet of the period. Later on, Dame Sitwell, whose poems "Facade" were set to music, recited them with full symphony orchestras. They were also highly alliterative and wonderfully well constructed in their sound images. Thus the "saying" of them was triply important.

When I advise an actor, "Be aware you are in a *saying* mode," it implies that he cares what his line does for the other actors' intentions and for the audience's continuing enjoyment and understanding as the event plays out. You are not simply floating your words out over them, expecting the audience to stretch for the meaning and catch it if they can. Sometimes, of course, you may be called upon to play the type of character who is supposed to chatter something like that. It concerns me, though, when all of the characters in a Shakespeare play start chattering as if they didn't care if their lines happened to arrive at their intended destination. Words are uttered, and the great images appropriately timed and phrased, but little of the timeless charm, conviction, beauty, humor, and terror gets said.

The physical rhythms of dramatic communication need to be as explicitly inherent and as excitingly believable as the motivating dialogue. This synchronization tends to occur when the words are said, and heard, and then replied to vocally and physically in a saying manner. Believability is almost totally based on audience certainty that the actor who is in character obviously received reasons, impulses, information, and motivations for saying the playwright's lines, with which he advances his place in the unfolding plot, so certain of all of his impulses to say his response and be equally sensitive to his next move. He is being informed and prepared to respond in a listening manner and be moved by reports that are truly and excitingly said. The impulse behind this understanding is felt within the actor's physical body, which in sequence transmits the whole emotional moment to the audience.

Cliché Movements and Line Readings

We are unintentionally receptive to what we see and hear on radio, television, motion pictures, the pulpit, and the stage. As a result, we absorb a surprising number of clichés which the aforementioned media seem unable to correct or eliminate, either in plotlines or talent presentation. A cliché is some unoriginal action that the actor says or does, an oft-repeated use of a tricky gesture, inflection, or phrase which has no particular pertinent meaning at the moment. It is a response extraneous to the scene, an imitation of something that we have seen other performers do, of inflections that we have heard them use.

When we give in almost unconsciously to the cliché, it means our concentration has been weak. We haven't challenged our creative selves; we haven't been very curious. We may even have made an assumption (one that is not wrong per se): that "there is something of the actor in all of us, and therefore we don't really have to inquire, study, or exercise to be called a proficient and attractive actor. We've been acting all day, and we'll be acting all our lives." But we have not allowed for the fact that art is selective. We produce a selection of a playwright's composition designed to achieve his convictions of space and time and events brought to life by a select group of characters specifically controlled to advance his thesis.

The power of theatre is that it is of people, by people, for people. It is a popular art, relatively easy to attend and easy to understand when it is well done. It is usually communicable and available, and most people go to it with less hesitation than to an opera or a symphony. At the same time the theatre arts techniques are somewhat hampered by the fact that because they tend to be democratic, people believe they can act, without ever having accomplished the discipline and training of, say, a violinist, a conductor, a sculptor, an artist, or an architect.

So the theatre is both blessed and cursed. It is blessed by its universality and its popularity, and it is cursed by the fact that in many people's imaginations, it appears to be easily attainable. On the other hand, there is no barrier to their ability to participate as an audience—and here they are the base of the whole project.

I have questioned young people considering a professional career, coming fresh to professional auditions with only minor stage exposure, why don't you begin preparing yourselves? Gain the fundamentals? You don't try out for the orchestra if you don't play an instrument, and you don't have an actor's body yet. You have a body, but it's not an actor's body, or a voice disciplined in the actor's techniques. Learn about your instrument—your body and voice—sing, dance, speak, swim, race, tumble, play in youth and school plays. Read plays and work backstage. Accomplish these and then attend auditions; there will be more point with which to make sound professional decisions.

People sincerely interested in theatre should read plays, individually, in pairs, and in clubs or groups. There is almost no other way to get over the feeling that plays exist as bookish closet dramas. If you read only a few they exist merely on the page, but as you read more, you start hearing sounds which form exciting and informative images instead of only seeing words. And the moment that the play begins to make sounds for you, then you're on your way. Read a play for your ears' sake.

I don't want you to settle for clichéd movement or line readings, which for the most part are cadenced and monotonous. On TV and elsewhere, we hear much cadenced speech; it rises and falls by half tones and low tones, as in the typical minister and athletic coach cadence. Many politicians are poor speakers who haven't learned to take the next step from the cadencing to a direct person-to-person vocal contact, talking *to* rather than *at* their constituents. When they look into a camera, they don't see an image of it as an interested, attentive person, so they cadence. The result is more sound than sense. The rising and falling of the voice comes from artless attempts to evoke emotionality. Many evangelists are masters of the rising and falling style: overcharged, overly rhythmical, overly emotional and headed for hysteria. Because they handle their audiences well, such highly cadenced speech is recorded in the ears of anyone listening. Aural memory of such speech can be a detriment to an actor's sense memory and eventually to the performance. Clichés are deadly in theatre; they indicate that the actor is settling for something less creative and original than she is capable of doing, to say nothing of the loss of contact with the other elements of the dramatic moment.

When an actor resorts to cliché, we often tell her to "re-read" the line, although I hate to use that term because I try to avoid the sense that we ever "read" the lines. We should be "saying" them. We tend to accept at the beginning a fairly bland, uncommitted saying of lines. There's nothing wrong with that when a play is being read—or said—for the first few times, when the basic events are new. Many times experienced and talented actors can create practically a performance-quality reading at the outset. We do have methods of teaching proficient sight-reading for maximum effect. But it has been my observation that often actors who are facile in their first readings do not invariably improve when the rehearsals begin to explore and enlarge the character relationships as the author indicates in the plot development.

How is a director to know whether a mature first reading is the sign of even better ones to come, or if that is to be it? I may ask the actor to come back and have a conversation, or to read some other scenes; all the while trying to discern whether she is sensing the basic plot or argument carefully, and trying to really hear the other actors auditioning with her.

In a first reading, little attention may be paid to the set and action details, which may be provided by the resident stage managers for the preparation of the printed commercial acting edition. Playwrights sometimes punctuate well and sometimes not. Under the influence of certain dominant emotions, a person might not bother about a comma at all. These neat little black marks on the page have relatively little to do with much of the characters' plotted conversation, which will be eventually inflected and informed, high and low-pitched, fast and slow-paced, harsh and softly sounded, according to emotional and psychological plotted demands.

To search for the sense of the lines, to say what the playwright intends (as well as you can discern it), you must take time. The sense develops with reflective thought, plus a keen aural contact with the intentions of the other actors. In speaking, everybody takes a split second, more or less, after listening, then hearing, concluding, breathing and vocalizing, to choose an appropriate answering word or phrase, affirmative or negative. That is what the playwright had in mind. He trusts that the actor has the experience and the technique to vitalize that line and realize its implications, the sense of it as well as the fact of it.

Perhaps the speech is one in which the character is deliberately lying in a very convincing manner, as in a courtroom scene. Then it becomes challenging and exciting for the actor to explore lines for what they don't say almost as much as for what they do say, and for where and how pauses might intensify the meaning. The experienced actor knows that in so doing, she is providing a pulse to the scene, as well as a convincing portrayal of the author's intention for the moment. This realistically human pulse can never appear on a printed page of the text, and thus it is that the actor becomes the co-author of the play, moment by moment. These instances are basically the only occasions when the actor becomes the top number-one creative artist of the project, for she takes over from the number one person, the dramatist. In general, she would have to be described as a re-creative artist-associate.

Initial readings sometimes have a tick-tock, metric-mechanistic pulse totally impossible to achieve in a living body: "And-so-he-said-to-her-where-is-it-you-are-going-and-she-replied-well-I-will-be-back-very-shortly." Such sounds are empty of internal motivation and human purpose.

The actor must know that externally and internally we advance according to rhythmic pulses of hearing, deciding, acting, conflicting, winning, celebrating: all of which are externalized for the involvement of the audience by the words of dialogue and the action of the plot, thus rendering a special experience, explicitly to and for the audience. These rhythmical pulses and variations flow in, out, over, and through our words.

Loosening the Ears

It is interesting to listen to actors, particularly young actors, converse among themselves before and after rehearsals. There is a noted vibrancy in the way they convey the experiences of life in and out of the theatre to one another. Indeed, there is a natural vitality and buoyancy in all heartfelt conversation, which is an activity central to human relationships. In general, the process of putting on the play seems to dampen this "inner" physical and vocal presence. If we are not careful, we can lose a large amount of this natural charm and vitality when we take it to the stage.

Some people who feel interested in acting get their first vicarious taste of performance from concentrated watching of TV or the movies. They absorb interesting exterior aspects of these performances, and a concept emerges: Acting, with a capital "A". It manifests itself as a somewhat superficial representation of how certain select persons behave and sound when acting. With television, more people have been exposed to hearing scenes played over-dramatically due to plot structures plus the director's personal style. These unsubtle styles of playing have to an extent been affecting incipient actors. (All of this comment is in reference to "pictured" acting, which is not always in close reference to *stage* acting, primarily because the stage requires perfection every performance; pictures do it over and over until it is judged perfect.)

In a large audition, there may be young people of various ethnicities and backgrounds with very different natures and points of view, with various strong points, weak points, and personality colorations. But regardless of these differences, if you make a recording, you may find a remarkable similarity of the same inflections on the same lines and situations. Even more notably, I have on many occasions conducted auditions for the same play in two different states in two different seasons, and have again recorded almost identical inflections for the same lines. How monotonously similar they all sound! Thus it has been proved to me that in almost all cases auditioners are very highly involved with their personal selves and do not extend their talent and experience into the "why" of the scene, but instead succumb to the "what."

Recently I have tried to anticipate this problem by simply reminding everybody that they are totally unique in themselves, and that this uniqueness is the origin of an interesting character on stage once it has become bonded firmly with the author's intent for the personality to be played.

Wherever their minds are, I try to divert their attention from the process of reading the words. I get them to focus on the fact that there will be an audience, hopefully a large one, in a matter of weeks. Even if there is not an audience at this point, they should imagine the audience that could be there overhear and enjoy believing in what the actors are saying. This is an example of aiming for the end from the beginning.

I also draw the actors' attention to the ideas and emotions they are acquainting themselves with at the moment, even on a first reading; and what they are responding to in the other actors, who are responding in turn to their meaning. I am more concerned that they listen with their eyes and hear with their ears. It is then that they will use their voices from where they live without affected diction they may have heard certain actors using. Right away, there is an excellent chance that a communication line is being set up with the audience on the basis of their being interested and eager to willingly suspend their disbelief and engage themselves with the fresh, enigmatic, magnetic personalities on the stage.

Immature actors' feeling of modesty, false or otherwise; of isolation, of being an island unto himself, are probably what produces this denial of personal worth and warmth. The spell these feelings create can be broken by "bouncing off the other actors" as they rehear him, listening critically—as an audience would—to the way the others are investing the playwright's ideas with viability.

I like to have auditions on the stage, as most directors do. There is a sense of the audience being seated out there. It seems to help some personalities who have an inner urge to express themselves but a lack of technical knowledge of how to freely release these urges. They need to feel how to move elements of their own personalities up and outward into the role; to find what it is within them that will contribute to the authority, intelligence, and charm of the character. It is the audience's presence—real or imagined—that can help one to do this.

As a director, I need to know as much as possible at the beginning whether I'm going to be working with a person who is sensitive to tone and intervals in the use of the voice. Early training in literary interpretation and poetry reading can help cultivate a higher level of vocal variety and sensitivity. Let us assume that casting has allowed me to evaluate an actor who is not satisfied with the mere hackneyed reading of the script, but has deliberately simplified her job by projecting and sharing the intention behind her lines with the audience and with the other actors in the play. Then I can hope to hear inflection, as well as pitch, rate, and force, arrived at logically.

Inflection comes out of a real need to be clear, convincing, informative, amusing, charming, and at one with the audience. It doesn't come easily out of a chapter on vocal production in an acting book. We know about inflection from everyday life. The ear is as important a sense organ as we possess. Yet for many people, to keep talking, volubly, montonously, profusely, is more exciting than listening well to another person as a source for what the next response should be. Once again: to listen is to perceive; to hear is to learn.

When a playwright sits at his typewriter creating the characters, what is in his ear? What controls his sense of dialect or syntax? How can we project ourselves according to his intentions? First, we spend a lot of time searching through the sense of his sentences. Then we need to relax and loosen our ears. Soon, the tones and tunes will begin to sound and we can begin our composition.

Positions and Oppositions

Many acting books repeat the old advice: "No movement without a purpose." But any actor can get so concerned about thinking out purposes, especially during the early constructive rehearsals, that she ends up with little significant movement at all. I try to give her another reason for movement by encouraging her to learn to locate the confrontations and oppositions in and around her character, to be creatively aware of them early on: the pros and cons; the black and white; whom she is for and whom against, and why.

This may seem mechanistic, but in practice it works: in everyday life the physicality of these oppositions is abundantly evident. In them she will find the playwright's physical and emotional structure for the play's progress. One person moves tentatively towards another, receives smiles and nods affirmatively, opens his arms. Another shakes his head, pounds for emphasis, and walks away. The simplest of movements contains cues and clues about the underlying attitudes, both pro and con. If she reads carefully, exploringly, contact the other actors, and she is aware of where she is logically positioned, then she will begin to sensitize herself to whether the playwright has posited her in the scene with basically affirmative or negative motivations and intentions. Has he sent her on a journey to acquire positive or negative achievements in the course of the play?

Those who are drawn to the theatre tend to be communicatively alert and alive. Yet somehow the qualities of affirmation that are implicit in what the playwright had in mind are to a remarkable degree dulled and neutralized in the initial readings and explorations of character. The same is true of negations. It is not important that the actor affirm or deny from her own personal point of view. She is playing a character, not herself. But it is fairly simple to intuit when a character is sympathetic to another character. Whom does she affirm or deny, and which side is she on? It is very helpful for the actor to be quite clear about these affirmations and negations, not only for the sake of her own characterization but for what she contributes to the other people in the scene.

As the play moves into blocking, regardless of

whether the director allows the actor to search out and find and justify his own positions, or whether the director has previously choreographed the production, the affirmations or negations in the body movement are totally expressive of the gradations of emotional status in the character. Most bodies are not clear or strong enough in their affirmations or negations to project these clearly to the audience. When the actor is in the experimental stages or has not been in a position to receive constructive criticism, I would probably urge him to more rather than less expression of these oppositions, just to bring the whole picture into sharper focus.

Do the eyes see or are they blind, so to speak? Do the ears hear or are they deaf? Is the character numb or full of feeling? Is the temperature hot or cold? Is a sensation smooth or rough? A taste sweet or sour? A smell fragrant or foul? These are all basic sensuous pros and cons common to the personal life of the audience and the persons of the plot. The playwright may not have been explicit with many of these basic elements of our being, but clues abound in the time and place, in the set's atmosphere, and the costumes' color, line, and fabric's mass and texture. You may always enrich the pros and cons with life's sensualities.

Is the body moving up or downstage? To or from other bodies? Is it moving fast or slowly? Presenting the front or back? Is its rhythm manic or depressive?

Is the voice high or low? Fast or slow? Loud or quiet? Smooth or harsh? Is its level ascendant or descendent?

These are some of the elementary physical and compositional oppositions—and the gradations between them—that the actor needs to be aware of and express through his physicality, from the feet on up.

The director may have projected the general spine of the play and the philosophy to be presented and explored. But a blandness often persists too long in early rehearsals, with nobody being much of anything pro or con, young or old, crazy or sensible, even though this is the time for the completion of experimentation in all of these qualities and relationships.

Obviously, in an important, complicated play of character relationships, one waits for an appropriate period of time for the subtleties to emerge. But the broad strokes of affirmation and negation should be there early. The author has chosen a specific location in time and space, and he has placed his characters therein according to patterns of opposition so that the story may be told in believable dimensions. As the actors learn to live the story, they internalize these oppositions, and as their voices come to express the oppositions, their ears start to hear the qualities and inflections of the voices. Thus the liveliness of the oppositions is firmly anchored in the minds and emotions of the audience.

III

REHEARSING

The Sense of Place

"Blocking"—the process of placing the play on its feet—is an odd term, that suggests "stopping" or "getting in the way" to many people. But it is really the first step in the script's words and action involving the actors' introduction to their new play space. At this time I stress an understanding of the place to which the actor is going to move before he moves there. A playwright, as he begins a play, has before him all the places in the world, all the times of day, seasons, years, all ages, all architectural scenic atmospheric details and styles. His options seem unlimited. The actor builds his interpretation by sensitivity to what choices were assigned to him by the playwright and why.

In everyday life we are affected all day long by where we are. The nature of the room we are in, whether a living room or a bedroom, an office or a back porch, shapes an atmosphere toward what we're going to agree or disagree about. In taking to the stage, we tend to be so eager to get the mouth working that we forget to be sensitive to the physical context for our motivations and behavior. A place can be dramatic in and by itself, in its location, its change of light, its dimensionality, and its plasticity. Pay due regard to these factors. The line may call for an expression of love or hate or fear. But what is the time of day and year? What is the atmosphere? What elements has the playwright chosen to explicate, support, and amplify his theme? If directors, designers, and everybody else connected with the play use such indications, they are amplifying the intended impact on the audience. If the actors create any less, they may well be introducing confusion and indirection—unconsciously, of course.

I will tell an actor: now for awhile we're going to

change the percentages of our attention. Let's place only about 15 or 20 percent sincere thought and energy on what we're going to say, until we get to know more exactly just *who* this person we're playing will turn out to be. Place 75 to 80 percent of the rest of your attention on *why* you are surrounded by tall dark trees against a turgid, cloudy sky (in the case of a tragedy or melodrama), or a drawing room full of designer's evening dresses and dinner jackets (in the case of a comedy or farce). I find good response to this device or method of enlarging an actor's sense of place.

Many years ago I worked for a summer theatre in a Western Pennsylvania resort area, and we had to move one play a week from an interior, proscenium theatre to an outdoor stage in the round for a second week. I had to devise a means within one rehearsal of changing the floor plan from one environment to the other. It was a great satisfaction to find that *Three Men on a Horse*, in which interior sets are important, made the transition beautifully; the actors allowed the quality of their close ensemble acting to flow out of a practiced and creative sense of place, not complicated much by the shift in stage or outdoor surroundings.

My beliefs are posited on a generous and searching study of the place which has been structured in the play, and how the times, places, temperatures, and moods come together to unify and simplify the excitement and intelligence of the scene.

Externalize While You Memorize

In the blocking period, the script can become like an outer shell placed over the actor, an outer envelope of instructions, advice, directions, words, phrases, and more which we have to penetrate in order to reach the other actors, who are in turn probably trying to reach us. It is at this time the actors, by maintaining eye and ear contact, should be giving each other the sense of the plot structure and character relationships, in terms of the present visual intentions, tones, insights, and impulses. If the book is a barrier that keeps us from seeing or noting what responses other actors are contributing, it blinds us from seeing the present status of development. It is time to move away from it—drop it!

We should try to be aware of the first time we drop scripts in the rehearsal, as to what we see and feel at that point. We should never hold scripts as such; they should be treated as properties. They can be teacups or cucumber sandwiches in *The Importance of Being Earnest*. Sometimes we can just toss them on the table, then move away from and back to them as needed, keeping in character. Treating the book in a casual manner helps us to make greater visual and oral contact with the other people and is a good way to minimize the shock of really dropping the book for the first time.

It is a hard step to take. We naturally want to show to the other people that we have memorized our lines, that we accomplished our homework. But we don't really need to prove anything to anybody. Memorizing has little to do with the quality of the production, except if it isn't accomplished creatively, cooperatively, pliably, and with only normal anxiety. The words should be deposited back in the farthest reaches of the memory bank, to be withdrawn at the right moment. Grab the deposit with a sense of instantaneous excitement, as though you are seeing and sensing the precious word-images for the first time.

There is something soporific about rote or metronomic memorization. The labor of memorizing can force the voice into a cadenced pattern of sound in a narrow range. The worst mistake is to pace back and forth, repeating the lines over and over. The ear records all that with amazing fidelity and permanence, so that the dead cadence we have taught ourselves is replayed again and again without much reason—and no rhyme or rhythm.

I don't mind a "blank" memorization (which is, for some, not voiced), or one without inflection, before rehearsals have started or become detailed. We memorize the words only, and not how they sound. But this works only with experienced actors, especially those in a cast with a mutuality of training and a background of several reputable successes. They will learn their lines, then move into a full shaping of the moves and emotions of the play from a joint creative point of view. There would be a type of repertory company which would demonstrate this technique.

In everyday life, our faces and vocal rhythms reflect a thinking process that leads to externalizing, thereby projecting internal thoughts and ideas to the audience. Many exercises and theatre games play with this process of thought projection, which at times seem quite successful when experienced in a concentrated class situation. Some of these games seem to suggest that if you concentrate long enough and think something, you'll project it. But it is actually the highly organized and sensitized personality who externalizes the expressions and the rhythms, the attitudinal movements of the head, facial muscles, the searching and answering glancings of the eyes, all the employments of the hands and the body, without being especially conscious of them.

For the body of the audience to receive, believe, and enjoy the idea, the idea has to be externalized. In the movies, where the camera is within inches of the actor, the merest dilation of an eye, or the flutter of a muscle in the face, can externalize the thought, due of course to the intimacy and magnification of the face and figure enlargement. On the stage, however, the small internal nuance would most certainly be lost, but the impulse for externalization is the same. On stage we simply use more of the same impulse, while being meticulous about vocal production and articulation without seeming to be. It becomes a matter of the actor's and director's judgment: under the circumstances, is the actor reaching her audience? The impulse to externalization should be alive even at the stage of the memorization of lines. The audience is ever-present and always should be.

Creative Listening

The ears are every bit as important to effective acting as the mouth—for a good reason, because the ears control the mouth—for that matter the voice as well. The ears, both inner and outer, are constructed for a more complex and subtle function—on a much higher level of intelligence, probably, than the mobile, munching mouth muscles. The ears are beautifully and almost magically designed structures, closely linked to mysterious brain impulses and controls. With all this fine equipment, isn't it stupid not to use them?

Many plays do play out a whole evening with very little evidence that the actors were listening to each other or to the atmospheric background sounds provided for color and mood—and as such not hearing them either. Integral to the listening response, there are very simple facial and bodily reactions, recognized by everybody since they are employed by everybody.

Ideally, reactions between the factors and factions of the planned plot happen according to a kind of simple, believable logic. If you are onstage and haven't any dialogue, and are listening to a long speech, or standing apart listening to a scene of two or three characters, the reaction principles are posited on not only listening but hearing and learning. That means hearing as the character you play would hear, and realizing that you are usually your own playwright, responsible for creating the other voice. Rarely does the playwright provide it.

Hearing implies an inner recording of the dialogue. It is a learning process: you are either agreeing or disagreeing with the ideas and thoughts you hear. Creative listening, during which you hear pros and cons involving concerns and interests, informs you; you learn important facts with which you can deal in the future. It is a matter of motivating body language at its most subtle.

There used to exist rules about listening and reacting on stage: never to move outwardly or inwardly for fear of distraction. As a director, I soon disagreed with that as a dictum. I found that one of the simplest ways for an actor to steal a scene is simply to sit or stand in rigid motionlessness. Then, all of a sudden, everybody is looking at her. "What's the matter with her? What's she doing? Has she forgotten her lines?" Her inaction creates an almost ominous feeling of distraction, out of the situation, even out of the play. (This is not to say that at times, in staging suspense scenes in melodramas and tragedies, that the ominous element may be well placed and affirmative in gaining appropriate tensions.)

On the other hand, if you have a fairly extrovertive actor, and he's listening and nodding a little too self-consciously, you have to say to him, "That was an excellent reaction. I think it probably began a little too externally and obviously. I'd like to feel you're agreeing to plotted ideas more than other ideas; in other words, choose your reactions, pro or con. Listen carefully, be open, and then respond." This idea is an important part of playing telephone conversations, the technique of which is rarely accomplished with complete conviction. Among actors who have played them well, the most superb examples which come to mind are Laurett Taylor, the original Amanda in *The Glass Menagerie,* and Jane Fonda in the film *Julia*.

When someone is saying something, and you are preparing to reply, the fun of it is seeing that you personally might react quite differently from the character you're playing. And by the simple act of judicious choosing, you begin to place yourself in an acting attitude. Creative listening is an art that carries right down into the feet. The foot can reflect boredom, fatigue, exuberance, and almost anything else in response to a long call.

Character development is a progression from one fact, one action, one bit of knowledge, to another. By the time the play is over the audience has come to know several facets of the character plus the developing relationships. The audience has been transported to a new level or area of understanding the issues. Actors should avoid jumping to that goal. Don't overreact early in the scene, when it is just underway. Instead, match the intent of the other actors; as you agree or disagree with them, stay with them as far as necessary, using only the appropriate levels of energy to capture your goals.

Your key for pacing yourself is in the other actor's next speech. You can gauge how strong you were in your line by how strong and argumentative he becomes. Matching the other actor doesn't mean copying his rhythm or tonality. It does mean a matching of intelligences of the characters you're playing, an interlocking of emotion and thought toward the goal of that particular scene. Often there's a clash of intentions, and you're going to win or lose. It must be clear to the audience who wins or loses, and often it isn't. The positive/negative alternating current must fascinate and convince them.

Sometimes the matching of the other actor has a physical aspect as well as a vocal one: the sense of threat or combat, the development of affection or rapport, the growth of separation, has to be underlined by action. To arrive at the physical actions, you gauge and study the body language of the other actor, and you determine what you can do next, either to protect or advance yourself.

This simple statement always holds true: to listen is to perceive. To hear is to learn, perhaps to understand. Think about it, expect it, and make it work out for your audience.

The Actor in the Grand Design

An actor should always be in a close relationship to the playwright. The playwright is giving the actor at least fifty percent of the dialogue: this is the dialogue that emerges, the speech, which helps motivate the fleshing-out process. But the actor is responsible for the other fifty percent: the inner dialogue that remains an unspoken action of the actor's mind and body.

The dialogue that originates within the mind doesn't need to be any less explicit than that which is spoken. It may be the exact source of motivation for a strong action and hence is expressed physically with double clarity.

This fifty percent, which is the actor's contribution, should be the exact reason he is interested in acting in the first place. Otherwise, he is not creating very much, but only *recreating* the dialogue, situation, and place. If an actor has accepted the challenge of the playwright's technical springboard, the springboard that has thrust the actor up into the action of the play, and he maintains it and carries it over to the next action, then he is responsible for a lot of "dialogue" that may not be explicitly apparent in the script. This, then, positions him throughout the course of the play with regard to its resolution and final impact on the audience and may well account for his present and future reputation as a viable, important, and reputable actor.

I try to help an actor find a comfortable entrance into the texture and structure of the play, an entrance that is informed as to period, style, and mood; fluid, not static, rigid, or stressful. The actor must listen well to the other actors in order to learn how he may build the construct, the logical "platform" that he wants to stand on to hold his own through the course of the story.

In the Twenties, when I was studying, we used Alexander Dean's book on directing and movement for actors. It served a good purpose in its day because it codified almost everything. It analyzed the play as a formal design, actually presenting a short course in pictorial composition, as if it were a treatise on landscape design or portrait painting. Many directors have commented that this rather rigid book is not a bad start, particularly for the sake of creating a common frame of reference and a common vocabulary. I don't think it's used much anymore. It is important, however, for groups of actors, with the guidance of the director, to discover that the play itself, its interrelationships and the evolving plot structure, constitute a *design*. The actor comes to understand the physicality of the character in the interplay of positive versus negative group movement. Then there will emerge a pictorial quality in his relation to the other actors, arrived at functionally rather than directorily.

This is important in the proscenium stage where all of the presentation is framed, and where, contrary to Alexander Dean, the most important acting areas are not always downstage center. There is a whole set of rules governing the relative strength of playing areas, none of which is wrong, but which are not essentially helpful if rigidly interpreted. In the natural course of stage events, for example, you discover that the right and left sides of the stage reflect oppositions between characters or groups. So do the up and downstage areas, and many times diagonals are even stronger—all of this dependent on the contribution of the set designer. The play in a remarkable way shapes its own course; its own picturization evolves. Certainly the physical setting, provided by the director and designers, should assist the actor's convictions about the place. The lighting should help him focus the mood, time, and locale. The actor needs to play into that light; not just because the light enables him to be seen, but because it represents a fact about the reality of place. Actors can and should be of prime assistance to the director, especially in large ensembles, in finding and playing in the most logical and available areas.

The physical levels of the set will affect the character relationships. The presence of the throne on an elevation implies the elevation of the king with respect to the common people. Towering, powerful people have to be played from metaphorical as well as literal levels which are quite different from those of other characters. A director works hard to bring about a simple, believable sense of their power and whether their authority is administered easily or with a certain amount of struggle.

Actors do have to know, particularly in ensemble scenes, where the center of the scene is taking place. They should know if they're in the middle of the action or if they're watching it, and if they are affirmatively or negatively related to the progress of the structure and argument of the scene.

The Third Dimension

The actor offstage is a living, breathing person of obviously three dimensions. The lighting artist has gone to great pains to light him and his areas purposely to stress his depth as well as his height and width; so has the costumer. The director has helped him discover the movement in time and distance. So how does it happen that onstage he may appear as a cardboard figure and sounds like one as well?

The first task for an actor approaching the playing of a role is of course to read the play several times in its entirety (and more for fun, if out loud). He does not immediately underline the lines and name of the role he achieved in auditions. Secondly, he imagines several possibilities of realizing the relationship of his role to all the other roles. The playwright has given some parenthetical directions and suggestions of time and place. Often actors will attend primarily only to these details when they would really find basic assistance in attending to supporting plots of all kinds, especially with respect to action and mood. The less experienced actor's initial approach to the role tends to be isolated, with the book in hand and the feet implanted.

It is often difficult to solve a problem in the acting process by oneself. Of course, to solve the problem one has to recognize the problem. To recognize it one has to distance oneself from the contained concepts of "I," "me," and "myself" as foremost in the process. Rather than upsetting that comfortable egoconcentric state, the tyro may cling to his first misconceptions, isolating himself from developments in the other actors' interpretations. In an expert company, with excellent talent, generous experience, and high technical standards, the actors will attempt to dislodge that isolation for their own and the tyro actor's present and future reputation as professional actors.

I will encourage an actress who is not growing in her role to add a dimension to her playing that is in essence her own individual, personal dimension. I encourage her to consider what the playwright designates as important to the action of the individual role. Then, regarding that as just two-dimensional, she takes a step further into herself, including her own personal attributes, her physical appearance, vocal qualities, and all inner convictions as well. The sum total contains a reason for the final casting and adds a new third dimension.

In almost all art, the goal is to achieve an added dimension in what is being achieved. The sculptor has a block of marble; while it has its own shape, within it he conceives an inner outline, a different shape that makes us aware of the block's full dimensionality. A graphic artist works with two dimensions, but with strategic use of certain hues, values, and intensities, portrays the illusion of lines, compositions, and textures. An artist begins with an obstacle in the form of a mass, and the measure of artistic success is determined by the way he breaks through it and realizes from it his original intention and dream. This is what may be called discovering the "third dimension."

With acting, the third dimension may also be found by searching for almost the exact opposite of the apparent prime aspect of the character. If you are playing a "villain," search for and hopefully find every opportunity to see what is not villainous in him. As for the hero, try to find some subtle and logical chinks in his armor. In other words, round out his character by looking at his other side. Every charming, compelling character trait contains the seeds of its opposite. If a character is very timid, pulling back from the flow of action, watch for moments when the natural germination of the action allows him to bloom assertively.

As we take our work through the building moments of the play, we should keep our convictions of the character fluid and pliable so that we may logically tint and shade them in response to the advancement of our associate actors as we interact with trust and truth.

Often one is cast within a prescribed range of height, sex, and weight. Beyond these physical characteristics, though, the actor has an awareness of his own potentials, both positive and negative. Hardly an hour in our day passes that there isn't a process of feeling, thought, and action running through us, which constitutes the pulse of our life and our believability as human beings.

It is this third dimension of our inner selves, which people may not see, that we should raise to the surface of the character, or "externalized." The third dimension can be touched. There are always possibilities in the character that are not rigidly determined, simplistic, or obvious.

We tend to wait for the great moments, the high climactic peaks of tragedy or melodrama, the soliloquies, to admire the actor's skill at balancing many factors. But sometimes we find oppositions of feeling in the more "gentle" comedies and tragedies. The great Russian playwright Chekhov is involved with three-dimensional characters. Well-played, the Chekhovian characters often flow back and forth between happiness and sadness in such a fashion that you become utterly fascinated by their rare individuality and humanity. In fact, if at a certain moment they appear to be fairly happy, then that is probably the time they are the saddest. And when they appear to be quite sad, they're often enjoying their special inherent sadness. You miss them altogether if you level them to a one- or two-dimensional playing.

In other playwrights, say, with the early Neil Simon, the actor often has to supply the rounding of the character, the sense of opposition and variation, since the author has not always given it dimension, comedic or otherwise. The characters as they exist in the script tend to occupy two dimensions. The actor asks: how much of the character may be played three-dimensionally? He can safely dare to set up an antithesis to the character as given, and by bringing the two together, give him the dimensionality of life. That human dimension is the colorful cloth, bright with feeling, woven through interplay with other living and breathing people.

Taking Chances Safely

There seems to be a frequent tendency, especially among young professionals, to arrive at a high tension of body and voice too early to make sense in the accruing of further events over the next two hours. They use not only the requisite energy to fully realize the author's intentions but add an uncontrolled and uncalled-for intensity which can be misleading in many directions.

A poorly prepared actor may not be utilizing all of his senses, particularly as he enters the play and the action. He may be playing too much from the surface. He comes across as being single-tracked, and simplistic in his attempts to think out the action and formulate the dialogue.

There are theories which advance the idea that one needs to prepare extensive research when beginning to develop a role: to record details of the historical background—the mother, father, aunts, uncles, and cousins—details which may or may not have any reference to the actual plot of the play or to the character as written. Many people in the business nowadays feel that this is unnecessary. Certainly there are plays of historical and familial content which require, at the least, research on the actual plotted points, but it is true that you can overdo the research aspect. As the great actress Mary Morris used to say when I was her office-mate at Carnegie Tech, "Do be careful not to think yourself right out of the role."

To get into the presence of the character, open up.

Be willing to absorb everything. Be vulnerable, be intuitive. Go with the character and what happens to him; go with the other people in the play, listen carefully, and be receptive. When the actor is proceeding through his course in the play—experiencing the character's relationships, his ups and downs—there is a pulse, a rhythmic lifelikeness to the acting that rarely comes about in any other way than by keeping an open mind. It may not come out of a reflective, thoughtful, analytic attitude. In many cases, a person of relatively limited intellectual ability can grasp the fundamental action quickly and successfully.

One of the observable points that differentiates the most vital professional actors from many non-professionals is that the professional has learned the techniques of "taking chances safely."

The moments of release, no matter how "large" or "small," provide the actor with decisions which, though already plotted, can be played with a supersensitive, intuitive stroke that he judges, at that moment, to be *right*—especially as it was presented to him by his co-players. A video recording may disclose some subtle changes from the previous night or any other night, but the "basics" are all there. There is a safety net in the sense of a basic structure of the character which, learned in rehearsals and performance, carries through into subsequent performances despite momentary "chances" that the actor may take.

The result is that the audience believes that the character is behaving intuitively. The actor's choices are spontaneously arresting and artistically convincing. Having discovered the character, he proceeds through performances in a series of rediscoveries, taking chances but always relying on his safety net.

This process is like injecting the mind and body with an activity-fluid that charges them with super-alertness, super-awareness, super-vitality, and super-projection of the moment. This does not mean that the resultant playing is loud, explosive, or chaotic. It may be exactly the opposite. Rather, it means that the underlying power is present, ready to be released in the time and place pattern which has been structured by the playwright and performed by the actors (with the guidance of the director).

If you are to play, as successful actors do, a demanding role over a long tour, you'll need to know how to "juice up" the whole body, mind, and spirit every performance. And you'll need to know as well how to control this energy appropriately for the nature of the character caught in the complications of an organized plot.

Giving the Dialogue a Second Chance

"Selectiveness is, for me, the most valuable lesson I have tried to learn over the years, and the one I most admire in the finest of my contemporaries. The truest test an actor must pass in sustaining a role over a long period of consecutive performances is that he is continually discarding every unnecessary gesture, simplifying every movement and inflection, so that he may eventually achieve the most truthful expression of his role at every moment of his creation, however often he has to repeat it."
—John Gielgud, "The Urge to Act,"
New York Times Magazine

Sometimes I will compliment an actor on a performance, saying forthrightly, "I want you to know that at this stage you're doing well." I say this knowing that I may be contributing to the actor's egocentricity, and that the next time the scene is quite probably not going to be as effective. But the actor's ears have heard him perform it well. The ears memorize quickly, and they know what is right. Once they have registered what sounds and appears as right, they will not settle as easily for clichés again.

When I compliment an actor after a well-played scene, I'm aware that I should compliment the other persons in the scene, because if the scene was affecting, nine times out of ten it was a multi-person achievement. Sometimes in rehearsal a scene may be so right that it rarely becomes "righter," even in an otherwise splendid performance. If such a marvelous moment happens in rehearsal, I don't care too much if a young actor doesn't achieve it again in performance. It will probably all return to him on the night of the show! He will have learned, no matter how briefly, the creative and advanced sensing of all that acting may become— with more practice, more refined rehearsals, and many, many more performances before varied audiences whose open critical reactions teach him directly and personally how entertaining he has now become.

I know directors who encourage overplaying in order to gain freedom and to infuse some breath, breadth, and vitality into the rehearsal; then they allow the scenes to settle down. I do that quite often. On the other hand, one can also suggest "underplaying" to place the importance of articulation and inflection, although one must be careful in using that word since it may have different meanings to different actors. There has to be some rather advanced playing to begin with before underplaying can make much sense.

When it appears that an actor is becoming locked into a superficial approach early in the rehearsal process, it's sometimes a good idea to suggest underplaying, in order to maintain the actor's confidence when suggesting re-evaluation and re-playing. This suggestion can bring in relaxation, his ears will tend to open up, and an aural vitality may take over for the "mouthiness." I ask: "Could I hear this a little differently? Try to *re*motivate, *re*read, *re*-evaluate, and *re*say the lines." Or: "Say it any way other than that last way!"

Sometimes actors fall into a type of idealized pattern that is quite serviceable for a few early blocking rehearsals, but which eventually becomes tiresome and lifeless. They may have learned their lines too quickly for fresh contact and informed motivations. As a result they are moving mechanically through the scene, not thinking about or feeling what they are saying to the others, and why. They may have derived cliché readings from watching too many politicians, evangelists, commentators, and commercials. Their lines of dialogue are not coming from thought, or from a need to answer what has been asked of them.

At a certain psychological moment—and the director has to know exactly when—advise the actor to "reread" his lines, which means in effect to re-listen, re-evaluate, and take more chances, while measuring the results against the ears' recording of the way he previously played the lines. What the actor has been playing is capable of a more convincing pattern of rhythms and tones. Being comfortable in the breadth of his early work, he can in the process of rereading simply eliminate a certain amount of unnecessary, obvious, and self-centered "acting."

I get the same result out of a device so simple that it sometimes upsets actors who frequently expect a much more complex and sophisticated device. I say, "Okay, don't act. Don't read. Tell me what the *words* are." So they tell me what the words are. When they *say* the words, they aren't merely saying them perfunctorily, for they already know who their character is, who the other characters are, and what the aim of the scene is. At that moment, the words will be so fresh and choice as to create convincing sense and thereby delight the ear. It hears something new and authentic, perhaps in tones it heard only yesterday at home, at work, in the street, in the rare fine production on television or on the motion picture screen.

Platforms—Physical and Psychological

If one graphs the rise and fall of action apparent in the structure of a play, one sees that the high and low waves of emotion have pivotal points of arrival and departure. The origin of these alternating currents is an underlying emotional status which I choose to call a "platform." The playwright structures the whole play as a continuous series of scene-moments, rising and falling according to his master plan of physical and psychological plotting. This vibrant energy "platform" is implicit in the master design of the play.

In the early part of the century, Russian "constructivists" incorporated in their set designs what was in a sense a graph of the play, with actual platforms and levels, constructed of wood or metals. Various areas were later painted in black, white, and a popular crimson. If a character fell from grace, he had a ramp to descend. The concept of the play as a structure was taken literally. Even today, one can borrow some of these visual concepts to help the visual dynamics wherein actors can clarify their relationships. The director, if the designer has provided him with a stage of several levels, obviously will use it to enhance the confrontational points.

Conceptually, the various platforms that are more or less implicit in the structure of the play are often realized in the basis of the floor plan which the scene designer creates, especially if she chooses to use platforms. We have long noted that in summer stock, with limited rehearsal time for multi-scene plays and musicals, plus group scenes of thirty or forty people, half a solution is a well-designed and visually logical set of platforms for actors to move onto, off, and around. Immediately they are forced to compose themselves as a physically and emotionally viable ensemble. Martha Graham often used dynamic and challenging set pieces of ramps and levels as devices on which to choreograph major movements of stress or conflict. Physical platforms are a way of challenging performers mentally and physically to create dynamics of opposition, relationship, and dramatic or comic contrasts.

The psychological "platform" concept is only a device to help clarify what is or might become a problem of status for actors until emotional lines and relationships come into valid meaning for them. Platforms can be springboards; they can be trampolines; they can be soft and squishy, depending on the intentions that the actors and director feel the playwright wants at a given time. For example, Greek tragedy traditionally presents heightened levels of emotion and tension. Satire on occasion comes along well by putting imaginary thumbtacks on the platforms, so people step gingerly with respect to what they're doing. In short, the concept helps actors *represent* their status, both in their relationships to the other actors in terms of the pro and con possibilities, and in their own progression in the play according to a graph of rising and falling emotional levels.

All the actors involved in the development of a plot structure should realize that each of them creates a part of the plot structure and the visual structure (which are one and the same thing). No one person is responsible for the whole presentation; there is a give and take. The level of belief that will motivate serious, violent, or highly dramatic action—a stabbing, or the striking of a blow—must be upheld by the composite group structure.

So we're searching for a "platform" from which the actors feel comfortable in playing a heightened emotion, or acting with a believable bodily status. Actors in the company of each other do arrive at heights and depths of emotional vulnerability from which their thoughts and actions emerge to take place. It is critical to their believability whether the "platforms" are high or low enough to make the action exciting, humorous, or believable.

Actors' relationships with the other characters constitute a pattern of "platforms" from which they can view the scene from other than a flat stage floor from beginning to end, even in the change of elevation such as sitting on a chair. There comes a natural awareness of the intentional stresses that the playwright has employed. The script suggests many aspects of the character relationships which enable him to position himself emotionally and physically with regard to the others. With a sense of such "platforms," the actors can quite readily hear the tonalities and energy levels suggested in the lines.

Often less experienced actors lack a sense of proportion about the relative importance of their role. A person playing a smaller role may overplay it, giving it a greater stature than the playwright intended, and consequently overlift the platform for the scene. Often in an exit, an onstage actor, instead of leaving the scene behind him, enriched by his function, will take the scene with him, leaving the people on stage with a lowered "platform" which they have to build up before the action can proceed. To correct these pitfalls, the "platform" concept may be explained to inexperienced actors quite reasonably, and it will help them not to lower or heighten the "platform" of a scene unless that is their function. When preceding scenes have built an elevation high enough, they can play "high" scenes with a relaxed awareness of the emotional levels demanded by the structure, which they are committed to, maintain, and certainly enhance.

"Aim for the End from the Beginning"

During my first year at the Northwestern University School of Speech, I had the privilege of getting to study with the prestigious old actor Otis Skinner. He was not a listed member of the faculty, but arrangements were made for a few of us to play small roles in his play in downtown Chicago and have informal lessons. He used to say, "All you young actors, set yourself up by projecting a modest confidence which says to the audience, 'I hope that you will like and believe me (and I know just how to do it).' But always be certain that as you play your successive scenes, you aim for the end from the beginning." It is a phrase I've borrowed through the years, and which many of my actors and associates have recalled, enjoyed, and agreed with.

Generally speaking, from the audience's point of view, the most impressive and important parts of the play are the first three and the final three minutes. In the opening, everything is promised: a style, a certain type of excitement, a movement towards a goal. In the last three minutes the promises should be fulfilled, so that the audience will feel when leaving that they're taking the play home with them. (This is as true in the modern experimental theatre as in the traditional "well-made play.") The director, technicians, and actors, should leave no doubt that what was promised has been delivered.

With first rehearsals, there is a natural attraction and challenge about beginnings. The atmosphere, ingredients, and energies are fresh and vital. Rehearsals go well and confidence permeates every pore. In the mystery of transforming a personality into another self, changing the present into another time and place, there is a spirit of experimentation which should be maintained until the unfolding situation begins to communicate to the audience. During this experimental period, there is a great comfort in going back to the beginning, "taking it from the top," which by a later time represents something fairly tangible, measurable, and committed.

I'm not minimizing the importance of getting started properly, but for every effort that is made towards an effective beginning, there should be the same or perhaps a doubled effort toward making an equally well-placed finish. Unfortunately, the closing rhythms, cadences, and resolutions are not always as fully realized or presented as the beginnings. Therefore, just as soon as the whole company is comfortably set into the demands and intentions of the total play, I may well run through it to the end, just as soon as I feel people know and can appreciate what the end demands of them.

The experience of the revealing, exciting ending solidifies the purpose of the whole drama's existence. Stresses felt during the mid-rehearsal periods begin to disappear and become constructive when the end of the play becomes clearly evident. We ask: what specifically are we leaving the audience with?—what color, what philosophy, what ideas, what excitement, what humor, what emotions, what theme? When, with early and thoroughly researched rehearsals, we can provide our best answers to these and probably other more specifically personal questions, we relax and settle ourselves into this informed challenge of constructing the play for the audience as the playwright intended it.

Even some professional productions may have impressive beginnings and listless endings. Actors on tour are often fatigued and can't quite manage to harness their energies to drive on to the conclusion. The last act must really tie together all plot strands and take the audience to a higher energy level. The actors must be up to this challenge. A trapeze artist may have to perform a quadruple somersault as a finale when he's the most fatigued—but because of a superior physique, hard practice, and alertness, he brings it off. Throughout their professional lives, actors find that some of their most challenging moments are in the third act. To bring the evening to a full completion demands years of conditioning and playing experience.

I have noticed that Shakespearean productions often tend to fall apart in the last five or ten minutes. The concluding dances and songs of the comedies, which may seem distant from modern tastes, are often dull—unsung, and undanced. Even in a really fresh and precise production of *As You Like It*, a tame little rustic song and dance at the end had the audience leaving the theatre let down. If there is a song and dance in a play I'm doing, they have to go into rehearsal the first week. They require an unquestioned surety of experienced performance skills. If they are so planned, rehearsed, and energetically performed, they can assuredly top and appropriately end the comedy.

Ongoingness

Directors, in the procedure of developing the scenes, should strive to *infuse* their advice, constructive criticism, and demonstration rather than to inform intellectually.

It is important for the director to prearrange the rehearsal plans in such a way as to be certain that there is a safe space for the play as a whole to recover from rehearsals. To advance into the final performance, to feel fully comfortable and in relaxed control with the ongoing, advancing tempo of final polishing, sufficient time should be scheduled before the so-called "dress" and the "finals." The play's structures should be mounting toward the intended performance in whatever mode the play is cast.

Otherwise, we have the all-too-frequent experience of witnessing on opening night performance another rehearsal (however proficient as such)—and, for that matter, it is possible to attend a closing night rehearsal.

The rehearsals are, as the name implies, a period given to re-hearing and recall of the experimental successes; they are a recalling of instructed details of movement or lines or working out actors' problems. The alert and efficient ear records necessary lapses in the continuity of the story line quickly and accurately to the extent that the actor may lose his sense of any lapse. The rehearsals must have ample time to begin a tightening process with due logic and control in mind and body. The recollections of the past directions and experiments are not now necessary and must not appear in performance except as a moment in the plot. A "rehearsal-type" performance is "acting backwards," still recalling past "business," advice, lines. A real *performance* existing in the present and future is "acting forwards"—no looking back, only creating an "ongoing," exciting, authentic, fresh, informing future.

The word "ongoingness" has direct reference to the ever-present obligation to muster all details of acting full steam ahead! Aim to enjoy and value not only the sense of ongoingness but also the sensation of it, a living, breathing progression of events, plot complications, character and personality changes progressing or regressing towards rewards or censure, and philosophical challenges advancing toward acceptance or rejection.

A lighter way of commenting on a similar artistic principle in music was made by the composer-performer Miles Davis. When asked what he considered to be a basic difference between black and white performers, he replied that the black is always a bit ahead of the beat, while the white is more often slightly behind it. His assumption was, of course, that performers are all involved with the ongoing rhythms, whether their expertise is achieved naturally or by training.

There is, of course, in the final stages of the production's development, a rather keen sense of momentum, but it is imperative that it be under varied degrees of vocal and physical controls. The energy supply is always monitored so as not to exceed what is clearly necessary to clarify and support the believability of the moments.

An Anatomy of Climax

There is a frequent problem of overacting or underacting the strategic moments of climax. There can easily be impulses from both actors and directors to overenergize early scenes to a height that does not give later scenes any available place in the voice and body to go for effective playing at a more climactic or concluding moment. As a director, you should select and plot the climax areas, and invent a private system of measuring the "heights" and energy levels. Reinstate the tried and true advice—"use no more energy than is necessary to correctly and brilliantly play the scene." Perhaps the light, set, costume, and sound designers will join you by measuring each climax in decibels, lumens, hues, values, and intensities. Proportion is another sound concept which comes to mind, whether producing classics, performance art, avant-garde, or burlesque.

It is all too apparent that with such areas where there are several artistic techniques called into concerted action, the chances for errors are that much greater. Since each climax results from differing accumulated factors, each scene must have its own color and character; each, its own energy level. Furthermore, the ages, nationalities, and temperaments of voices constitute racial tonalities, dialect rhythms in simultaneous responses of pro and con sonority. Complicate these ingredients by the facts of presenting comedy, tragedy, farce, melodrama, or other less pedantic modes. Each mode is by definition composed of inherent instrumentation, from typical timbres of saxophones, guitars, trombones, clarinets, flutes, snares, in sync with antic, burlesqued, chasing, falling, dancing, tumbling, hiding, disclosing body movement; or cellos, violins, oboes, harps, basses, and tympani in sync with decorous, controlled, statuesque, graceful, powerful, beautiful body movement.

Climax is present in the lives and times of the inhabitants of the interesting places where these modes are the models of all climactic actions. So what is likely to happen in the plot-line and action in the country of farce? When your play inhabits the country of melodrama, what plot-line and action is possible or even probable? How will the playwright rearrange the events to provide a sequence of climaxes which excite and frighten, but which, having provided momentary thrills, will preserve the hero and heroine for posterity? These multi-complex peaks of confrontation form a truly important platform on which the viable action is dependent: the definite "business" required, such as physical skills, firearms, swords, boxing, or wrestling, is rehearsed knowing what impact is planned for the audience. Exactly *plot* all climaxes in every necessary detail you can possibly summon. Ask for advice and guidance of specialists and *chart* every detail. You will need to check back in the closing rehearsals as you begin to leave the rehearsal for performance just to verify if you plotted correctly at the beginning—and to readjust the energy levels.

As an afterthought, keep on advising on the energy levels during the run of the play. Nothing upsets a well-proportioned play like an inadvertent news, radio, or TV review, especially if it appears before the next performance. When the cast knows ahead that you will be checking energy levels at each of the first ten or so playings, you will find a greater and an easier way to preserve your original structure and at the same time enjoy the enlarging "chance-taking" on the part of the actors. They will feel safely anchored at all strategic spots of climax. They will safely fly together from platform to platform, setting down at last for a well-earned curtain call.

Since some productions require large-scale casts at climactic moments, additional actors (unfortunately listed as "extras") are trained to function as persons for or against the protagonists. Just a word about the training which also applies to the supporting main cast actors: do not give up much, if any of your major "spine." In crowd movements, keep your fast or slow character foot and arm gestures. Keep your basic vocal levels, intonations, volumes. Not everyone will agree with the disputed conditions. Argue with those about you, win or lose your point, and *never* fall into the prevalent situation of taking on the vocal pitch and body gestures of the group, or you will end up with all of the banal conviction of an opera chorus. Indeed, the critical moments of the major crises offer the group actors excellent challenges for creative contributions to the play's success. There needs to be a splendid admixture of high and low, fast and slow, loud and soft, tall and short, old and young, pro and con, with everyone "taking chances safely" to create and maintain spur-of-the-moment believability.

When the propositions of the plot approach a climax, supported perhaps with some appropriate sound effects, lighted either realistically or non-realistically consistent with the selected design details; voices then come into a relationship with both sound and light, and movement enters in. Each element by itself does not necessarily have an impending or impressive function. But the orderly accumulation of elements does support and build up a climax. It is a matter of orchestrating the elements of color, light, and sound that are being thrust together in full sensuous support of the acting, while maintaining the integrity of each, in order to achieve the playwright's intentions as to the relative pitch and power of the climax.

If, in the exciting execution of this theoretical climax, there is an increase in rate of the body responses of one character against another, almost inevitably everybody accelerates at about the same tempo, lines tend to be rushed, and foot movements all seem to be built on the same underbeat. Actually, this or almost any climax can't happen that way in "real life." There are people who respond to circumstances slowly and others who respond rapidly. Portraying any climax with this disparity (and others) notably enhances the truth and the hoped-for excitement.

When a crisis involves a fight scene, the director must create what the playwright often doesn't provide in the script: the sounds of stress and injury. In a surprising number of productions there is a disparity between the visual and auditory violence; they don't mesh on stage. One of the most difficult scenes to stage is the complicated fight scene in *Mr. Roberts,* where you have a lot of husky sailors in a regular knockabout brawl. The choreography needs to be meticulous. It comes down to helping establish each person's own basic tempo, and basic timbre or quality of sound. This is one of those times when all the elements should be very strongly administered. A thorough interweaving of lines, action, dialogue, thought, and movement is called for, in contrast to times when the feeling is light, thin, and delicate.

Playwrights, as well as actors, can drift toward

cliché techniques as they approach a climax. Both playwrights and actors often embrace too many details, thereby taking too much time to advance and too little time to recede. The receding has to be in proportion to the height of the climax. If you study the real psychology of sorrow and fear, you learn of this universal tendency, and then you can avoid the cliché. Climaxes need to be approached *technically* so that it is the audience who should be led to grief, pity, fear, sympathy, and, in rare moments, to catharsis.

A proper climax reveals a human crisis as a vibrant, living experience intended by the playwright to liberate through the struggle and thereby release the audience.

Incarnating the Character

As one contemplates the character within the play during the incubation period, how closely should one want to place the mind, spirit, body, and costumes of the character on oneself? And how soon?

Many actors disembody themselves quite successfully; they are able, technically speaking, to sit at the back of the audience and view themselves as on stage, in the action with the others, on the set. There's nothing wrong with this: it's a kind of second sight, like experiencing that which you have created and then looking at it objectively. But I do think it wise to advise them that they may be directed to change when the other actors concerned develop their concepts. For many people it is a constructive viewing experience. But when one gets on stage, if one isn't careful there can exist a type of disembodiment of viewing and playing the character as if outside of oneself. The effect is that the character is not really personified or totally present at the moment.

I'm rarely certain how totally or thoroughly actors are willing to go towards incarnating a character. Not that they have to do this, unless it happens to be their gift—as Hal Holbrook goes into Mark Twain, with total authority and an almost superhuman sensitivity to the character of the role. (He has amply illustrated, however, that his talent is pliable and entirely capable of creating a rather wide range of ages and personalities.)

A talented and thoroughly trained actor gathers up all the cues and clues he can from every source— through a wideness of inquiry, questioning, listening, and observing, from which he attempts to select and organize in the creative company of the playwright, director, and the other actors. Being comfortable in the breadth of the early work, he tries on various emotions for the judgment of himself and others, and saves the singularity of the character as almost the last thing to be developed. When that singularity comes, it is probably the impact of the quality of the other actors in the scene and not of some strongly dictated self-image.

The Actorly Ego

Actors naturally tend to bring a good deal of self into the rehearsal process. While appreciating the individuality of an actor's self, a director should provide extension of thought, ideas, and influence to what the self is aiming for, what it wants, and what it is or is not capable of achieving. It is occasionally obvious to the audience that in some touring professional productions, the characters seem self-serving and coldly self-involved—and not because the playwright wrote them to be performed that way.

I have been, on occasion, necessarily frank with actors and advised them that they displayed an ego-concentric attitude, which tends to build a shell around the character. It's as though each enlightening set of fresh convictions born of the rehearsal has, instead of creating a revelation, tended to conceal. The intention to *reveal* has somehow not been allowed to extend itself or to break through that shell into the time and setting of the play, to the other actors in the scene, and through them to the audience.

The path that has to be traveled from the moment the author conceives an idea to the moment an audience thrills or laughs in response, is often interrupted by stumbling blocks known as concentric egos. Yet the ego, when directed to the shared accomplishment of performance art, is not a detriment. People involved in all the arts are there by virtue of strong, vibrant, creative egos. Some actors seem to extend themselves selflessly to others, while some withdraw. I often use the word "concentric" to denote the rigid, hard-edged, and boxed-up ego, as opposed to the valuable, important actorly ego which is malleable in its intentions and feelings.

It seems particularly difficult for young people to extend themselves, which is understandable, since one begins at birth with total dependency and self-interest. The whole process of growing is one of learning with other people. By college age, one has still not quite emerged, certainly not as evidently as when, with marriage and children, the outer world becomes an exciting and challenging reality, and the extension of the parent for his family, friends, and enemies hasn't even then run full cycle. The problem then is how to present that journey as a full cycle. It's a tremendous challenge to be played with by the director, playwright, and associate actors.

One simple device has helped: I tell young actors that as we develop the play together, we are obviously on our way, advancing in a newly chosen direction. We are launched on a journey. Perhaps off in the distance we can't see the final objective; it's off over a hill. Presently we find our way up to the structure, but the door is closed. We learn by using certain legitimate technical devices to unlock the door, hoping to enter the world of the play's structure—the time, place, and people. While we are still informed about it we are peering through and prying open the door. Very often the door will close in our faces. Perhaps by experimenting with other devices, other emotions, other relationships, or simply by rereading the play with enriched appreciation, we can now open the door and enter happily and confidently into the world of the theatre place, breathe that special atmosphere, speak that beautiful language, and experience the emotions of the fascinating persons who live and love in that particular country, place, age, and mode.

At that moment we are in a position to confidently and daringly bring the audience with us, inform them, guide them, and excite them. We can unite actors, designers, and technicians, each with their own colorful convictions and personalities, and conclude with a minimum of selfishness and a maximum of giving. Every acting book I know describes this as "vulnerability": the willingness of an actor to open up, to be totally available to the audience in all the requirements of the play and its plotting.

Opening the Door

In the early rehearsals, the role is "over there," out of the book, and you've got to get close enough to it to begin the process of recognition. But how to achieve the completed physical and mental details seems to be a long trip to the future. You willingly accept the services of an experienced, trained guide. Together you soon discover problems to solve: difficulties of the speech, complexities and confrontations of the plot, obstacles within yourself—and all these in close contact with the other personalities involved. You solve as many of these problems as you can along the way in rehearsals, with the aid and advice of your travel guide, the director.

When, by the mid-rehearsal process, you have mastered most of the "tour plan" and "arrived" at the play structure, knock on the door with a confident and competent fist, and expect entrance. You take a deep breath and the door swings open enough to step into the play's space, and meet the people who have preceded you so far. This new experience may seem to have only momentary reference to the work you achieved at the beginning, because the work is or should be partially assimilated. You push that aside, you meet the new characters here in the new time and place, you respond to them, and they respond to you.

It's all on a level of fresh, alert interplay, creating a pre-played game, complete with rules, a special field, uniforms, and critical spectators. Ideally there is little that appears artificial about it; in fact, in the best productions there might seem to be no "acting" at all. It is much like an infusion of timely incidents and timeless emotions.

Rehearsal now represents a work/play period of joining with others to discover and deepen channels for action and communication, which can be wide, quiet, deep, turbulent, circuitous, or very direct. They are the courses through which the characters will eventually move and emotions flow. Superior performances depend on urging your character to relax and flow down the channels you've created for yourself in conjunctions with all the others.

Once, when I was producing *The Taming of the Shrew* during a residency, I learned rather late after my arrival that most of the actors were music majors, inexperienced in theatre. A few weeks later we had reached a point advanced enough to be relaxed in rehearsal, and we were standing on the threshold of the play, outside the "door." With all of the work we had done, we were about to begin to have twice as much Shakespearean fun with it. But it was necessary to create an opening, an actual stepping into the play-space as Shakespeare may have viewed it. He was cueing us to see and feel it with more insightful definition and just plain communication: to meet and become involved with the people of his creation and the circumstances as they occurred. So I asked the actors to judge for themselves as we opened up the first scene: is this any different from last night? No, it wasn't, they concurred. "All right, let's go back and now knock on the door that's not quite open enough to allow an easy, free, boisterous access, take a big breath, and when you feel that you have essentially absorbed the soft Italian air, bounce up, open the door wide, walk in, embrace each other, and 'play it.' "

Then it happened. They were in, around, under, and on top of it. It was partly a tightening up. But the main point was that the lines were being *said*. Faces brightened as they literally recognized each other's new characters, and their ears *heard* for the first time, instead of only listening.

I wanted to keep the rehearsal at this pitch, so I told my two assistants to gather all the other actors in the cast, some of whom were studying scenes, to come in and see if this fresh momentum would carry over. The next scene didn't quite "get there," so I advised the actors in the first scene, "All right, *you* talk to these people. You were there. You're in this area, familiar with this country, this city, these streets, and this slightly foreign tongue. You've opened the door. You're on the spot of action. You bring them in. And I don't care what you do with them. Welcome them, shake hands with them. Bring them in with you to experience the atmosphere, the group language, beliefs, tastes, and pleasures."

So they helped each other. It was the scene of Petrucchio's first entrance. Petrucchio was not experienced, but he was well-voiced, well-built, intelligent and industrious. He caught the change in attitude right off. He was relaxed with the sounds of Paduan cordiality in the fresh voices confronting him that rehearsal as compared to the night before, he instantly responded. The actors had understood that they were no longer, in a sense, sitting in the library reading the play, no longer sitting in class. The way had been prepared, so they could open the door to the play's structure and place, walk in, breathe the fresh atmosphere, and live their new lives for the next few hours in Padua, together.

After the Fact

By "after the fact" I am not referring to the legal term. This is rather a stolen phrase I use to describe the desired state that you as an actor, with the help of the director, are trying to attain, and from which your words may emerge with maximum meaning.

"Before the fact" you're on the path, along with the other actors in the scene, studying, preparing, and learning. "At the fact" is when you reach the door, assured of your preparation. When you have opened the door and walked through, you're playing "after the fact."

The "fact" is whatever is evident at the moment—the text, the business—that which *has to happen* at that moment. The "fact" is the moment: the dictates of time, place, circumstances, and the nature of the other characters' presence. As you approach the fact, you know that at a particular time certain words have to be said and actions taken. At any given moment on stage, the audience cannot discern that the present fact you are handling has been prearranged or premeditated—but of course it has been thoroughly prepared. It is played, however, *after the fact,* as though that were the only way for that character to act and react.

Proficient acting is always "after the fact." You work up to the fact, absorb and select significant factors from the material, put it together, learn what is intended, where you have to be, and even what you wear. Then, having accepted and assimilated all that, you play it "after the fact"—or, more accurately, "after these facts."

Every actor tends to arrive "after the fact" at different times of rehearsal. Much depends on the nature and accuracy of the casting; the difficulty of the play, structure, mode, and style of production; the length of the role; and the problems of memorization. Part of the director's everlasting challenge and dilemma is to assist all the actors in emerging at approximately the same time in the rehearsal process. The memorization and blocking takes place "on the path," on the way to the door, and at the door actors are faced with the fact as to what state of assimilation they have achieved. Then they have to open the door to the play—and into the performance prepared for the audience.

To be able to play "after the fact," you really submerge yourself in the text and rehearsed action. You not only look at the fact but see it; not only listen to it but hear it. You take chances *safely,* based on the facts learned on the road to the entrance. You do not record or memorize a pre-performance. The words are placed back in your mind wherever you store them; then out of the reconstruction of the confrontations you have established with the other actors, you in a sense re- improvise, as you might do in everyday life.

During any rehearsal, open yourself to involuntary action, especially to intuitive impulses, derived, of course, from related facts. Then consult with your director as to their inclusion. We get so involved with voluntary actions that we forget how charming and revealing involuntary ones are, rarely acknowledging them. Small, brilliant, dark, insightful, comic, revealing character colorings embellish and support human warmth in the confrontations of the play.

The professional actor, by talent and experience, knows how to take all preliminary steps more or less by himself, without losing awareness of his interaction with other actors. He still doesn't know exactly the number and nature of the nuances which the other persons are going to contribute, and the other persons do not know exactly what *he's* going to develop. His thought is how large, how deep, how firm he need be to support the other actors' emotional pitches. He trusts the others to know how to support his present and future status. He knows how to selectively control all the elements of extension, both psychological and physical, at the same time being aware of the relative proportion of his contribution to the scene, act, and total play.

Doors into the Play

"The theatre, strictly speaking, is not a business at all, but a collection of individualized chaos that operates best when it is allowed to flower in its proper medley of disorder, derangement, irregularity, and confusion. Its want of method, its untidiness and its discord are not the totality of anarchy it so often seems to be but the natural progression of its own strange patterns, which sometimes arrange themselves into a wonderful symmetry that is inexplicable to the bewildered outsider."

—Moss Hart, *Act One*

Long ago, I had been undecided about the way to achieve the sense of a bright tempo. We were in summer stock and always involved with straw-hat comedies. In the summer it was hot, and in order to keep people's attention you had to keep rehearsals and performances moving. There was a strong tendency to say, "Speed it up." But nothing happens when you speed something up except rapid speech with a probable loss in comprehension and articulation.

Occasionally an actor can achieve any rapid tempo with equal precision, almost as if he turned a record to a faster speed. Years ago, when a recording of *The Importance of Being Earnest* with John Gielgud, Dame Edith Evans, and other famous British actors and actresses was wanted, it was said the play would have to be cut to fit the record. The reply was, "We will not cut it, we will just simply play it into the time limits." The result is a pure delight. They achieved it with the inbred, inborn awareness of the mode and medium at which they are the most accomplished, and, of course, with superior speech discipline.

Back to the straw-hat comedy. It finally occurred to me, as it does to almost every other director (I was slow, because in the early years at college I had no experience in farce), that a main ingredient in farce and comedy which motivates laughter is *logic:* first the median line, then the response to it, and then the "payoff." If one doesn't respond and laugh, one doesn't perceive the logic, comic or otherwise. The comic inventions are just as funny with slow-spoken people as they are with medium or rapidly-speaking people. The speed of the lines doesn't necessarily create the humor; in totality, the humor is in the comprehension.

Now, I was not for keeping the audience sitting for long, and I don't like acting which dwells on details aimlessly—that's the opposite side of the proposition. So I told my cast in the comedy: "We start with a point to make. Call it a 'fact.' In rehearsals, we figure out how to lay it out, and I'm going to try to make it live physically, first of all. Physicality is so much a part of comedy; in a farce, it's almost everything. It can even be unrelated, if deftly executed; it need have only momentary plausibility. You physically have to project into the audience your characters' being, voice, manners, appearance, and personality. If anything, enjoy creating called-for eccentricities, but be believably eccentric. You plan to look like somebody I would enjoy hearing tell a joke, speaking clearly and comically, and whom I'm curious about. I want to hear what range of inflection he has, and I want it to be orchestrated in the comic tonalities. Then people will *hear*—in the mode of comedy or farce. Exude good nature, get the energy up, and *take your time*—the time the character should or would take in delivery and response—to be articulate about every comic line that is being performed."

When these actors took their time to play the logic of the humor, they were playing "after the fact," and the result was funnier and faster. But the way I got them there was not to *say* "funnier and faster," but instead to go back to the basics.

When we're "before the fact," we lay the groundwork by experimenting with what the playwright directs us to do and say. We strive to study and understand the lines and action which we assume will lead us to the believability of our character. We must be comfortable with our decisions. By the time we're dropping the script, hopefully we and all of our associates are "at the fact." We'll sound and appear confident with it; not awkward, artificial, or uneasy in any scene. But we won't yet be extraordinary. Now, in the theatre we are in a world that borders on the extraordinary. We are generally with slightly unusual people, with fresh things to say and do. As pretty ordinary people ourselves by comparison, we have to be careful that we don't reduce those extraordinary qualities about our characters. Yet we must communicate to the audience as being not necessarily aware we are extraordinary.

(The exception to this is those instances when the

whole play revolves about remarkably unique people and plots, in which case the lead actors are presented as an extraordinary challenge, as in *The Elephant Man, Equus*, and *The Miracle Worker*.)

We have become comfortable, as we have opened the door and walked into the play; we are in a confident and hopeful state of rudimentary safety and surety. And we are beginning to understand performance accomplished by playing "after the fact." The fact of our "safety net" almost totally surrounds us, and we have woven and knotted it with all of the meticulous work of the early rehearsals. We've positioned almost everything and tested it with the facts, but now we are beginning to play "after the fact." We are beginning to initiate the proper performance pitch. The fact is always right there like an oncoming wave. We ride right over it, and then we are on to the next fact, riding that one too with buoyancy, rhythm, and excitement.

I have found this idea very helpful in the playing of Shakespeare. Study everything meticulously, make it work, warm it up, and physically do everything in your imaginative world to embody the physicality of the characters, especially the women, for they seem rather muscular in body and mind, active, and bright. Project the archaic word meanings to the audience, even if there is little chance they will clearly know them. By your attitude and inflection, you can take that ancient word or phrase and translate its intentions. If "the fact" is ahead of you, stride up to it, take hold of it, and then guide it into the present context.

The early rehearsals are involved with finding the way up to the structure. The middle rehearsals are for learning to inhabit the structure along with the other actors, and for studying the logistics of the whole proposition—the causes, effects and purposes; the sounds and qualities of humor, the excitement of melodrama, the seriousness of tragedy, and the absurdity of farce. We test the color, line, and mass in the set, costumes, light, music, and sound. The late rehearsals constitute the process of taking appropriate chances—of making the obligatory transition from rehearsal to performance—so that when the audience arrives, they are there "after the fact," along with the actors. They feel a part of this world that has been created for them.

Thus we have produced theatre and thus we have earned our livelihood.

IV

PLAYING

Bridging Rehearsal and Performance

How do you, as an informed and experienced director, control your procedure in rehearsals so that you gradually make the transition into performance? How do you relate to the factor of an audience which is there to experience a performance, not a rehearsal? Unfortunately, many hundreds of audiences throughout the country are unwittingly viewing dress rehearsals, and very good, well-timed, neatly dressed rehearsals they are—but they are not *performances.*

One tested, reliable plan to avoid this embarrassing problem of bringing an immature work to the paying audience concludes that actors, designers, and directors may well profit from the breadth of audience opinion while still in the early rehearsal process.

In my first years of theatre work at the Northwestern University School of Speech, there was a distinguished professor by the name of Theodore B. Hinckley who was at that time the editor of the only magazine that seriously treated the theatre outside of New York. He asked us always to keep a notebook on hand, to draw a line down the middle of the page, and on the top of one half to print "pro" and on the other "con." We were to continually develop our awareness of the total impact on us and on the rest of the audience during all of the many plays we saw, of what we liked or didn't like and why—then to write our judgments in the appropriate columns. The point was to set up a private, personal way of acquiring candid and educated opinions.

The school made it possible for us to attend all of the major professional plays in Chicago. We also attended the early regional groups (Northshore Players, The Black Cube Theatre); we participated in Winifred

Ward's Creative Dramatics, played "extras" at the Goodman, and finally major roles on our own NU campus. These were great experiences to know large differences in audiences from both front and back of the proscenium. On each event we chronicled our attitudes and opinions via Professor Hinckley's "pro-con" plan.

We tried the same exercise with respect to our own work hoping to become more experienced and less self-conscious while judging. We concluded that actually, we tended to underrate rather than overrate ourselves. If you're involved in an acting class or group, try making up "pro-con" sheets and handing them out to each other (with the instructor's permission, of course). Ask them not to sign them but to comment constructively pro and con on your performance. Then absorb especially the concurrent comments of all of these, because the major source from which you can learn the array and variety of truths is the actual performance, from the audience.

In the theatre you cannot survive entirely on your own affirmative opinions unless you support and bolster them with a live audience made up of many opinions—many pros and cons along the way. Otherwise, talented people can become overflattered, and if there were bad habits acquired and not made known—which is possible, since it is a complicated business when you are your own instrument—their work is, of course, less than the best.

For many years I have brought in interested, experienced theatre buffs for the rehearsals along the way (preferably early ones), their only price of admission being that they will fill out a sheet of pros and cons of how they judge it's going. They do not sign these. It becomes nothing that will wound egos or anything else.

There are theatres that do invite people to attend rehearsals, perhaps other actors in the community or interested theatregoers, so that the actors, almost as soon as they've left their scripts, have an audience.

Thus the performance sense begins to evolve by itself out of the rehearsals. That bridging from rehearsal to performance comes about very normally and very naturally.

One might get comments to the effect that a particular moment seemed original and fresh and resulted in being very well "said" (pro). Maybe a line reading sounded forced, or a scene between two people needed to develop more elasticity (con). Respondents are encouraged to frame their own vocabulary and reactions.

As the director I will base comments on learned expertise, weighted perhaps by early audience opinions. One of the most valuable aids is in checking audibility in various areas of the theatre, assuming the use of the theatre for practice. I might comment that the energy levels have to be re-evaluated. We're "shooting off too many sparks" too soon, and as a result, when the next climax approaches, based on the pitch they have already reached, the actors are going to rip apart both their throats and characterizations. Other experienced advisors might have different reactions to such a problem, or express themselves in an entirely different way. They might say, "They're yelling, or screeching, rather than expressing the depths of anger" (or the slower development of painful disillusion).

As a director, if I received those affirming comments, I would know for a certainty what needed adjusting; I would work with the actors to motivate them into a more logical and personal relationship with each other. I probably wouldn't tell them that they were screeching. I'd suggest, "Use only the measure of energy that is necessary to convincingly play the moment, to make the point which is derived from the temper, tone, and tempo of your character's being."

Recently I broached this idea of soliciting early audience reaction to a graduate student in directing, and she was quite fascinated, so I suggested, "Well, why don't you try it with your next play?" And she said, "Oh, I don't think I could have it ready enough for them to see." So she had missed the whole point. It's not having anything "ready" at all.

Where I have used this plan, I have invited former actors, technicians, writers, critics, supporters, students, teachers, dancers, and all those who are "members" of the parent theatre organization. You need them early in the rehearsal process. (I've been asked into a number of final rehearsals, but by then it's too late.) Newcomers to a theatre group often join to participate as an avocation; such an activity is attractive, contributive and socializing in the best senses. The basic period of participation is for the *first* three to four weeks, the incubation and first words and first steps. Oversensitive actors may tentatively object. Why? Do athletes of any age or experience not expect sportswriters and observers, and not value spectator support?

Our theatre guests are in every way contributors to the projected success of the play. At the early rehearsals they are instantly introduced to each actor and technician. Subsequently associations and friendships are made. We are developing an informed audience as well. All members soon lose the "guest" status and become ambassadors to contact and inform neighbors and business associates. Later the "P&A" committees welcome them.

Rules are simple and sensible: no personal remarks are aired until after opening night, indeed no meaningful opinions are even possible after only two or three weeks of blocking. No free tickets are expected or extended. Final performance-type rehearsals are available as a matter of interest and pleasure of being a participant in the process. Some community and regional theatres provide special recognition to persons who have faithfully served in this process of attaining excellence.

The strategy is to aim towards performance as soon as feasible in the rehearsal process. Some actors tend to "perform" sooner than others. Rather than try to hold them back, I encourage the other actors who are rehearsing with them to confront them and share questions with them, to play back, as accurately as they both can agree, with the impulses they receive. Sense which actors are developing more rapidly toward performance, and use them to bring the others on.

An important technique which the director instills in the actor is the ability to evaluate an acting situation entirely on his own initiative, to structure an inner sense of what works emotionally and physically, and what doesn't—an evaluation. The simple joy of proving that you played your role on the team to your best ability is the reward—not what your friends say about you or what the newspaper writes about your performance. The goal is the selfless projection of other selves whom the playwright has chosen to delineate in a plotted story.

How Not to Have Fun

"I don't get a feeling of satisfaction out of the theatre nor do I ask for it. I get a feeling of life. I don't want to get satisfaction. I don't know how much any artist really enjoys and relishes his work—it's simply a matter of life when one's working and no life when one's not."
—Lawrence Olivier, quoted in
the *New York Herald Tribune*

If the word "play" naturally connotes having fun, it is understandable why some people assume that the purpose of producing theatre is to have a good time. I was attending a meeting of a group of people who were getting together to consider the development of a theatre. It was stressed over and over that if we get together we're going to have fun, and it's no good if we don't. And the fun must be dominant in what we're doing in all departments for all the elapsed time.

I don't suppose it occurred to any of them that this attitude might not be all to the good. Certainly they ignored the question of whether the audience was to be having fun too, and if so, how best it might be produced.

"Doing" theatre can be exhilarating. We who long ago chose to make it our lifetime profession certainly enjoy acting, and, on a more informed level of excitation, directing. The word "play" is tied into the concept of action, as in the "interplay" of a game like football or basketball, where there is recreational combat, a practiced sport of skilled interaction which wins or loses against equally talented, trained opposition. The rules of the game present limitations and obstacles; the golf course is designed to present hazards, the baskets their limited size and heights, the tennis net its impermeability. To win, you have to summon an agile mind and body, compete at times against odds, and play with others who are equally involved with satisfaction in team achievement.

In the theatre, there is the obstacle of the script, full of someone else's words and convictions. There is the need to reproduce accurately a personality type of an age and a manner of speech which may not be your own. One obtains an exhilaration upon finally winning against these odds. To the group that just wanted to have fun, I said that I did wish them exhilaration, but added that experiencing something of the pleasant sweat of the athlete in training was also very much a part of the total experience.

I have sometimes seen people strive to be in a play who really didn't want to; they were just helping out or pleasing a spouse. And it was no fun at all. One needs an attitude of giving. And "play" so often doesn't bear the connotation, particularly with respect to the theatre. That action involves a spirit of generosity coupled with a willing vulnerability and warmth. There is a measure of fun in it, together with discipline, criticism, repetition, and cooperation.

"Fun" too often connotes that what you do is to get up a group of people, pull the play together casually, and put it on for your own enjoyment. In such an instance, it's not a very constructive or considerate experience, simply because an audience, that fundamental member of the institution, is not invited to enter into the concept.

For a group interested in theatre activities, in order to enhance their enjoyment, their playing ability, and their legitimate "fun," it's very important to have a home for their audience and their facilities—literally, a theatre of their own. Many theatres are so bent upon personal fun that they tend to lack the will to put up with the realistic stress, the problems of finances and the minimum basic labor demands of building, renovating, and maintaining a theatre for themselves. The real fun of the theatre comes in its communality and in the stimulation of the family relationships which exist in a home. The theatre gathers together a close community of artists, plus the widely varied personalities of persons interested in the business and technical aspects, the managers, the musicians, electricians, dancers, singers, composers, tailors, ushers—and, of course, the fundamental presence of a continuing audience. A play is made *by* many people *for* many people.

There is but little fun if one is not apt in the theatre—that is, comfortable, convincing and believable. If one does not succeed, theatre can be painful for those in the play, not to mention those in the audience. So theatre has a potential for being an unhappy experience if that audience has not been involved in the aim of the play. The audience is the be-all and end-all of the play's coming into a viable existence. The personal fun of the people in the play is that of sharing the company of other talents basic to the theatre arts in producing legitimate dramas for a supporting audience. An actor immersed in "having fun" displays an isolation of the personality, a separation from the play, from other actors, and certainly from the audience. An actor need not be concerned over whether or not the audience is going to like him as an individual—only as the author intends the character to be liked or disliked in his plot ensembles.

Many years ago I played a minor role in a play titled *One Hundred Years Old,* in which Otis Skinner played an old Spanish patriarch, and we were all his many progeny—sons and daughters, grandchildren, and great-grandchildren. Through little acting lessons during rehearsals, he spoke to cast members and developed the ensemble. He was available to all of us at almost any arranged time during a lapse in the schedule. He was a devout lay reader, and he read a simple service on stage on Sunday mornings. His authority was spiritual as well as professional. He gave us a valuable key that had come to him and evolved during his early days in stock companies, based on ideas from a number of other great actors who had been his mentors. It concerned the approach to getting ready for our evening's performance: to say to ourselves, "I hope you (the audience) will like me—for I have enjoyed all my working and rehearsing—and I now think I know very well how to make you like me." What he was describing was how to take the stage with a kind of admirable simplicity, while suggesting that by a study of our craft we have mastered the art of conviction, which we exercise as an essential of the art of acting.

Playing Precipitatively

You do have to reinfuse the play every single night. You do not play the play tonight that you played last night, because the audience is not the same. To play "precipitatively," or intuitively, is to hold the material you have developed in your role while playing out of, into and with the other persons who are in turn infusing you and playing out from and into you.

The solid, creative director wants to engage the actors to remain pliable so that they reengage each other constantly. This is another way of saying one of the oldest truisms of the theatre, "Always maintain the illusion of the first time." Doing this successfully depends on being able to play the text accurately and creatively, at the same time being sensitive to audience reactions and accurately "reading" the audience response.

The point is that if you are playing only according to recalled memory of past rehearsals you have had, you have to, at the present time, be playing "backward." If you instead are playing in the immediate relationship to the other characters, you are anchored with them as they are with you, to the mood, the facts, and the playwright's intentions for advancement, you are playing precipitatively. You are playing "forward" out of the present moment, taking chances while safely anchored.

Yo Yo Ma is the only musician I've seen who "acts" with his instrument and his fellow musicians. It is proof of the daring of his style that in his mid-thirties he is considered a premier performer in the musical world. When he was teaching performance at Tanglewood, the words he used throughout were "advance, progress, infuse," which he credited to theatre training in performance. Before he goes on, he said, he drains himself of all breath, every bit of breath, and then moves onstage at the peak of a deep inhalation. This has been a standard performance technique in acting for making a first entrance which I was taught fifty years ago. It is like getting up on the precipice and jumping off but taking care of yourself, taking chances safely, according to the "safety net" of what you have learned in the discipline of rehearsal. You are then trusting that this ancient technique will assist you once again to attain your *performing* pitch.

Each time you perform, do not be timid about reinventing your performance—remaining, of course, entirely within the outline of your intent, purpose, and all physical and mental relationships with the acting company.

Enjoy stretching, reaching out in all outer and inner sensory areas. This supports and encourages the senses of movement outward and onward. You and your partners are getting onward—progressing. "Smash" inwardly the same way you return the ball playing ping-pong. Take these "safe chances" partly to challenge your partners and expect their returns with a sporting (playing) sense of competing. Always you are reasonably protected by the safety net of the playwright's controls. The rules of the game encourage and challenge the spontaneous playing of competitive ideas and relationships.

I especially enjoy Yo Yo Ma's demands of a young conductor accompanying him in performance: "Create enough to challenge me. Do not create a wall. We will engage happily in an art-fight."

Of, By, and For the Audience

"The appreciative smile, the chuckle, the soundless mirth, so important to the success of comedy, cannot be understood unless one sits among

the audience and feels the warmth created by the quality of laughter that the audience takes home with it."
— James Thurber, in *The New York Times*

The play takes place in the audience, which is the center of the play. It is a good and necessary force which also will guide you, compliment you, teach you, and reward you, and when you evidence selfish, undisciplined, egoconcentric attitudes will quickly and unreservedly punish you. That center, being composed of many individuals, is a multi-faceted creature. How do you get inside the mind and heart of this many-headed entity? Not by trying to please everyone!—which may result in pleasing only a relative few.

The first way to simplify the problematic answer is to make certain that every sound, action, and visual detail you create can be readily seen and heard by the majority. Assuming that basic communication is presented and established, you create the author's intentions specifically designed to appeal to the varied tastes, interests, curiosity, beliefs, and convictions of the audience, through the tones and overtones of the voice and body. All these technical aspects are structured by the playwright in the script. An experienced audience may pick up on the subtleties immediately, while others less experienced will be challenged and may respond more quietly and slowly. This presents a challenging problem for the actors, which they must learn to accept.

If the audience is a heterogeneous group of young and old, representing many levels of education and experience with theatregoing, the actors will key their pace and energy to that audience. Thus the actors will preserve the philosophy, mode, and frame of the play, but be able to alter their delivery if they sense that they are playing too rapidly for the empathic response of the audience. They should be able to modulate or control the tempo and still keep a properly coordinated vitality.

One of the best examples that I have had of this was in producing a handsome, articulate production of *Playboy of the Western World* at the Dock Street Theatre in Charleston, South Carolina. On opening night, there was relatively little laughter. Afterwards, a wonderful, aristocratic Charlestonian lady said to me, "Mr. Sydna, I just have to tell you, I just could not quite absorb that play. There were all those interesting Irish people talking and shouting and I could not quite understand all that. They were saying and doing at such a rate! We don't feel the need to have to work so hard on this"— which made sense. It was the first play I'd produced in the South. I said, "Thank you, Miss Alice." I knew I had made it, in that she called me "Mr. Sydna."

Then I said to the director and the cast, "We've worked hard to develop the unity and clarity and authenticity of this production and know where we're going with it, but just loosen it a little bit, and forget some of the advice you heard about playing through the laughter until you learned where it was. Forget the fact that you ever heard the term 'tighten up.' Now let's just loosen it up." And the next night it all took care of itself. We played probably three minutes longer out of holding for pure laughter.

(The Southern ears were long tuned to the more leisurely, softly enunciated—and charming— Charlestonese. The slightly adapted Irish lyricism was actually quite at home—for, many years ago, I was told that the son of famed English playwright Richard Brinsley Sheridan shipped to Charleston, and for a part-time vocation has been reported to have taught diction, which in that day was titled "Sheridanian"— still taught in certain social circles.)

The actor trained to consistently play with articulation of body and voice will hopefully have had enough jobs in his career, with enough audiences, to be able to explore and play the sensory qualities of the assigned roles under any reasonable situation. The theatre is almost by definition a sensual institution, playing constantly on the senses of the character within the play and the senses of the audience. The actors must be able to alter in this regard any night as needed. Prevailing weather, for example, affects the audience response. If they are outside in the summer, you hope they are relaxed and cool, with no mosquitoes or rain. If inside, you depend on air conditioning, an efficient furnace, and comfortable seating with suitable proximity for sight and sound.

If actors are to be successful, they must soon learn that "projection" is not a matter of loudness, but rather of sensuous warmth—"energy"—and contact, with resultant believability for the audience. From the director's point of view, these are elements that are related, assisted by, and developed by the "esprit de corps" of the company: the way members of the company believe in each other's abilities and techniques, learn to act and interact with and for each other, and develop a mutual dependability on each other.

The grouped response of the full audience is greater than the sum of its parts. When you're attending the theatre, you're another person during the course of the play's action. You tend to believe in a simpler philosophy, you're inclined to be much more patriotic, and you love mother and apple pie. You respond much more readily to sentimental material and laugh more easily at naive elements of plot. Around Christmas you fall into the mood of the eternal *Christmas Carol* and *Nutcracker Suite;* and so as well with other yearly celebrations. There are distinct seasonal attitudes, for some people love summer moods and times, others spring, fall or winter.

At best, attendance at the theatre tends for acceptance of many attitudes, aided by the facility and even the beauty of the playhouse architecture; by the excellent sight lines, realistic acoustics, and the comfort of the chairs. If you're cool, they warm you; if you're warm, they cool you. Then, having adjusted to those attractive factors, there is the reputation or nature of the play, designers and technicians; the influence of the playwright; the warmth and excitement engendered by the actors—all of these unite to promote the willingness of the individual to become submerged in the common feelings of the audience for the space of two or three hours.

If you are a bit disinclined to laugh at particular elements of humor in the play, and if the people all around you are laughing generously, you gradually succumb and soon you're probably laughing as warmly and frequently as they are. Even an empty seat near you makes a difference in the impact of the full-house psychology. One tends to enjoy being a participant, as part of the audience, in a successful play with famous actors. The impulse to join in the communal enjoyment is generally quite irresistible.

The whole production is designed to engender in the audience the willingness to suspend their disbelief, and as a result, accept the facts and fancies of the play as well as the relative stylizations which may be supporting the production. That is how the success of the play is measured, whether it is a Shakespearean comedy or a modern sociological tragedy. When the audience is willing to suspend disbelief, the actors must know how to reward them. That is part of the bargain made between the audience and the magic that takes place on stage.

My student actors have known what it is to have a director stressing their beginnings and their endings, and saying in effect: you must have organized your energy, never giving more to the scene than that scene demands, never giving more to your character than your character demands—but when the demands are great, you give greatly. You play with generosity and control the level of your character. Does yours have a primary, secondary, or tertiary level of importance within the structure of the immediate scene and eventually of the act and the total play?

Discipline is involved in playing intelligible, articulate ensembles—which is one of the arguments for repertory training. You play the lead this afternoon; tonight you play a spear-carrier; tomorrow you play a supporting role; the next day you play the lead again. Learn the proportions and the levels of the characters' function, and then their proportionate emotional pitches and stresses, always to the end of sharing with the audience your awareness and willingness to inform and excite at the proper time and place.

The obligation of the actor to the audience is to play the structure as it is designed by the playwright—as it should be played; to not confuse them by giving primary importance to a secondary theme. That is a challenge, particularly when in a professional situation you are playing different audiences with different attention spans on each night, sometimes adjusting to their varied degrees of attentiveness.

Above it all, always retain that transcendent sense that the audience is the most important factor in the total sum of theatre production. Their approval and disapproval will teach you what you're doing right or wrong, and will pay your salary whereby you live in your art. They will teach you what is moving or not, funny or not, and how to play tragedy, comedy, melodrama, farce, and all the stages in between. For the audience is the be-all and end-all of what you're doing; and you, in turn, are training audiences to appreciate and applaud fine acting in fine dramas.

Stage-Centered Plays

"Stage-centered" plays are those where the author's thesis presents slices of life in a selectively realistic style, and they are usually at their best when presented as such. Their intimacy and quality of interaction give the audience an insider's point of view. They are really looking through a wall of the room or a pre-selected site near the action outdoors. The message/story is extended to the audience by offering the opportunity for them to overhear and look into the intimate surroundings.

In this type of play, the actor feels fully that the largest percent of her attention rests on the other actors, and when she moves toward or away from the audience, she does not acknowledge them in the visual responses of her eyes or face. She moves from one area to another and literally does not seem to acknowledge the audience during the transitions. The audience shares in the explicitness of her body language and of what she's saying or doing, much as a "visitor" who has paid for the place of vantage. (Other productions will alter this discipline considerably.)

Many directors feel that some of the modern classics—Chekhov, Williams, Ibsen, for instance—may be played with this degree of control and intimacy. It is an accepted fact that *total* realism is not physically possible, although many of the most interesting theoretical practices in playwriting, staging, and design during the past century which were actually performed (such as Belasco's plays and productions) were directed toward a believability on a level of total realism which approached what is frequently defined as naturalism.

In this selective realistic style, acting places a premium on the actor reacting to the other actors, which means playing "off of" and "into" all the other actors with sufficient energy that the audience feels included in the developing confrontations. The audience chamber is essentially an extension of the stage's living areas. The audience members are not made to feel like voyeurs. They do not have to strain to hear what characters are saying or to be made to feel they shouldn't be in these intimate areas. Quite to the contrary: they should be empathically drawn into the confrontation and invited to respond emotionally and intellectually.

In this fairly difficult relationship to the audience, it is the director's professional responsibility to define and establish the opposing currents of aesthetic distance and empathy. Both are important in order to create a rhythmic flow between the action on stage and the responses of the audience. They are to be pulled into the emotional action, engaging their empathy. Then to an appropriate extent they are pushed away, creating the aesthetic distance, the rhythmic ebb and flow of human emotions, invariably provided by the playwright, and unfortunately, it seems, rarely recognized by the tyro director.

There is an elastic tension between the need for empathy between actors and audience and the need to recognize and play out the aesthetic distances which the author constructs. The essential flow between audience and actors demands the actors' positive awareness of the points of separation vs. the points of rapport, in order for them to be able to play the most pivotal moments of the total production.

It is the alternation of empathy with aesthetic distance, a projection into and pulling away from the audience, that constitutes the tide of the essential rhythms of being alive and kicking!

There are times that the actor will find that the playwright commands him to pull away from his audience with an idea, a movement, or an image. This should be an explicitly structured and organic situation, and played as such. The play is alive and breathing, with an intake and exhalation of breath, a pulse of emotional pitches, and a pattern of blood and brain interactions. The flow in and out of dramatic situations is charged with the crises and denouements of physical life. In the best-written plays, the playwright, through sensitive character relationships, establishes the empathic moments and the aesthetic distance which are logical and necessary for the full satisfaction and appreciation of all participants before and behind the footlights.

Audience-Centered Plays

An "audience-centered" play, like a stage-centered play, is always posited on a connection and interaction between the characters on stage, in vocal, physical, mental, and spiritual dimensions, and the ever-willing, supporting audience. But in the audience-centered play, the actor's position is usually more rhetorical, with a consciously composed arrangement of positions; singly and in concert the physical relation to the setting may be more formal, even suggestive of an historic tradition. The audience-centered play takes into account the audience's presence as an auditor and at times participant.

In classic Greek theatre, when speaking to thousands of people in a great outdoor arena, the actor possibly had to project more or less megaphonically, positioned directly facing the audiences. The structure of the Greek drama was choric and poetic, focusing first of all on the protagonist and the choric leaders. Later, single actors were added, who, with the aid of masks, played several representations of superheroes, heroines, plus a whole panoply of good and bad gods, many of whom supplied the personnel for confrontations and as such played the antagonist's dialogue. Shakespeare's was also an audience-centered theatre, playing on the projecting outdoor forestage, almost center in the colorful, closely clustered crowd, allowing the longer speeches and the more ornate poetic passages to be seen and heard. There was a naturally conducive atmosphere of lively physicality in the florid, ever-changing scene.

In the audience-centered play, by developing an attitude and a technique that brings the play formally and forcefully forward into the audience, the actor learns that he acquires both vocal and visual power when he faces frontally (which is technically termed "frontality"). In the opposite case of a modern romantic plot, one thinks of the hero and the heroine in a musical comedy—obviously devoted to one another, standing well downstage center, and facing the audience while singing a dialogue of mutual devotion. The actor playing many of the classic styles such as Molière and Shakespeare may employ frontality, as indeed he may have to when delivering the "asides" or soliloquies, the 17th and 18th century's style of projecting thoughts and fantasies. But the actor develops a technique of not allowing this frontality to leave him and land in the audience's lap. He exercises facial control, staying mentally with the characters that are beside and in back of him.

With the development of the theatre arts, this is not an unusual technique. In television and motion pictures, actors face directly into the camera, as if to other characters, while speaking to people at the side of them. It involves a certain mental discipline of not allowing yourself or your consciousness to escape you, keeping the sense of contact with people to the sides or in back of you. This is in contrast to the soliloquy, the lengthy expression of a thought or feeling, which very often is directed to the audience, but in which the actor still speaks essentially to himself. It is as if he has a self before him with whom he communicates as he develops the course of his thought.

Often with insecure productions one can sense and observe an uncertain vacillation between audience-centered and stage-centered styles. Occasionally, over-ambitious actors at an early level of success, playing in a stage-centered production, have gradually altered their plotted business to favor the downstage areas, closer to the audience, and therefore placing themselves in an intimate, ingratiating rapport with the audience. This change can be shattering to a carefully played scene nearby. The designated "style" of the play, which is in itself difficult enough to define, let alone to actually achieve, can be violated by someone's selfish ego trip. While the individual ego is fundamentally important to the actor and to explorations of the character's ego being prepared, fine acting has no use for the ego-concentric actor who displaces the proportions and balances of the plot relationships.

Consistency of style is a virtue, of course, for it clarifies the whole intent of the playwright. If it is conceived and composed as an audience-centered play, let's have it consistently that, including the designated sets, costumes, and lights, which have had to be approvedly designed to inform the audiences of the period, season, time mode and environment necessary to full appreciation of the performance.

Various "isms" related to classic realism are generally associated with the stage-centered production. Lighting in a stage-centered play should have the morning, afternoon, and early evening sunlight approximately realized as to angle, intensity, and hue, whereas with the audience-centered play, lighting might reflect character relationships and resultant moods without respect to time of day. A good example of stylized or non-realistic stage-centered lighting occurs in *The Glass Menagerie*, where during an argument between the mother and son early in the play, the playwright's stage direction specifies that an "angry orange" should begin to suffuse the scene.

In the first three or four minutes of the play, the director and the playwright conspire to promise the audience what it is they plan to convince them of—the place, time, season, and the country, period mores, and mood, utilizing all of the communicative arts in theatre technique. Then they stay with their premise. They stay with their contract with the audience clear through to the final curtain.

Many young playwrights will say, "That's too binding, that's too defined, limiting and dull for the present and future audience, that's too academic. I'm going to write a play in which I'll experiment, alternating so-called styles, incorporating variety in any imaginative mode which advances my viewpoints. After six or eight scenes in which the focus changes, the effect will be kaleidoscopic." Certain avant-garde plays seek to break strictures and structures. But one has to know what the rules are in order to break them, and know what one does to make them work for the impact on the audience before one can splinter them to let new air into the old forms. One still may learn about form, impact, and responsibility when one fills the contract at the end.

On Air

In my graduate student days, while studying art with Grant Wood, I learned to apply the hue over some very expensive, specially constructed rough paper called "Whatmans," if I recall correctly. I learned to lay the hues over this bumpy paper lightly and dryly enough for the spread and the hue to register, but allowing the little white flecks of the paper to show through. Wood described this simple technique as "letting air in" to the hue, gaining the vibrancy of the white undertone, while stating one's intentions with the dominant hues. He said, "Don't scrub it. Lay it on over the indentations."

In the same way, a playwright, as he "hears" the dialogue he writes for his characters to play, may hear also the air around the words which is needed to allow them their needed share of oxygen, thus to guarantee them lifelike sense and conviction. Within actors, too, there must be a generous supply of air underlying the vocal delivery in order to play the length of a scene, an act, and the entire play.

Too frequently with inexperienced people, the self-inflicted goal is to memorize the words so soon and so well that they can recite them, as they say, "backwards and forwards," or very rapidly and tightly, which means little, if any, air has been let into the speech, and almost no sense, mood, conviction, emotion, or logic can possibly emerge through the barrage. It's like a compacted package of words, all wrapped up and dropped on the stage. Sometimes, particularly with exciting plays, they fall into a vocal torrent of tumbling words with the rhythm of a rattling machine-gun bombardment of words, which can instantly generate an unintended comic effect.

Playwrights may not necessarily indicate pauses in their characters' speech. They intend that the actors study and sense the emotional and intellectual motives of dialogue. The actors embody the moments with the pauses of breathing air into emphatic ideas and emotions.

These moments of airiness develop in a realistic or semi-realistic way wherein we meet each other's requirements as communicants, with enough air-time for listening and responding, and for exchanging ideas and thoughts. Rhythms are the essence of our breathing, sensing, responding, loving, and hating, which all too often on stage lose their rhythmic believability, charm, grace, and beauty. They become hard and metric, the sort of effect we create when we want to portray a type of non-human mechanism, an automaton.

The same metaphor of air is true for stage movement. It is implied in the rhythms of nature, our inner rhythms which we feel with each heartbeat and breath we take, the rhythms of ascending and descending joy and laughter, of sorrow, and sadness, as with the keening of the Irish and the singing of rituals among many other nationalities. It is breathing the rhythms of life, the acceleration of good news or the deceleration of bad news. It is being poised in the amazing quiet of a terrible tragedy, until the body has a chance to comprehend and readjust itself to releasing the rhythms of sorrow and grief, and the sounds implicit in crying out.

I try to advise all actors, soon after casting and as they unite in the early rehearsals, to begin the structuring of who they are, why they're there, what their tasks are, what each is planning to achieve, and who's going to win or lose. Their answering words need to be felt out and breathed out as the playwright might well have heard them, so as to become viable and believable.

You can feel the air in the way people use words in their everyday lives, with degrees of color, emphasis, and flair. They stretch the word out; technically it *rides* out on the vowel sounds. In acting we try to reproduce that quality of conviction by holding onto or stressing key or important words, giving them their due *values,* because this seems to make the situation a little truer. Certain of the wonderful rhythms of the Shakespearean dialogue demand this approach. That's why when we teach the concept of word values we use Shakespeare scenes and soliloquies.

Sometimes there is too much air between words, as when a long, empty pause leaves the audience suspended rather than in suspense. This is the other side of the coin. Pauses incorrectly analyzed and motivated halt the ongoing thought and mislead the audience. On this, actors are advised to experiment as deemed to be necessary. They will come to a director for an opinion on their phrasing, timing, or rhythms; then they'll experiment with each other and finally with an audience.

Often in the releasing of emotional climaxes, words become too rushed and rhythms are too clichéd. The moments of denouement, the construction of climactic conflicts, are the points at which the playwright is aiming his story-line and philosophy. The most exciting moments in the play, when disclosures come about, are sometimes the most poorly played, from the audience's point of view. The actors seem to understand and to play well all of the constructions that build up to it, advancing and developing all details; and then when the point is ready to be dispatched, spontaneously and excitingly, it just isn't available or believable. Sometimes there appears to be a fatigue factor or a last-minute lack of control.

Note that the trapeze artist, with all his technique and timing well-practiced and assimilated, saves his new triple or quadruple somersault for the climax of his act, when he is the most fatigued. But he has learned how to conserve energy, using exactly enough to safely execute the earlier feats, pacing himself through moderately difficult maneuvers, so that at the climax he can attempt the most difficult task triumphantly and with energy and air to spare.

Entrances and Exits

The playwright to a large extent devises his structure on the rhythmic patterns of characters coming on and moving off the stage locale at various appointed and strategic times, not unlike life. An entrance is *made;* it doesn't just happen (though when well acted it seems so). The playwright has created a unit of thought and action on stage, a scene with a beginning and end, out of which a fact has emerged, a proposition has been made, or some part of the plot has been projected by the characters. The scene comes to a natural close when the given number of actors on stage changes. Perhaps a person exits who has to leave so that those remaining can say what they must say. Or perhaps another person comes in, changes the interpersonal chemistry, and we have a new scene.

This traditional type of division of a play's script according to entrances or exits has long been called "the French scene." In movies and television this scene is still the unit of rehearsal, and, frequently, of production. Often in melodramatic or tragic plays, the change implied by such a transition may be sudden or frightening. The shift into and out of a scene affects its color, size, shape, and mass, perhaps bringing in a new color, a new motivation of light, and a brighter, more dominant key.

As an actor, it is always interesting to study the varieties of motivations which the playwright provides when entering or leaving a unit scene he deems necessary in order to arouse and grasp the audience's attention. We must respect the fact that the audience's attention span is finite, so we constantly invite their interest by deftly creating the changing development of logic, moods, conflicts, and progress of the ensuing scene.

Thus an entrance designed by the playwright for the actor is a moment of special importance. The actor must come from somewhere specific with apparent intent. He doesn't merely wait backstage, timing carefully so that with a certain number of beats he can open a door, step into the sight-lines, and start his speech without a noticeable lag. He must make it evident that his off-stage experience has actually happened and that it has altered his progress.

The actor, to be a positive and progressive factor, must come from a definite offstage situation into the present on-stage situation. Preparing for an entrance becomes an integral part of an actor's technique, particularly if he's been offstage for awhile. Let's say he was on thirty minutes before, and the reason for leaving was given, that it was time for him to go and meet his great-aunt. If she never appears later onstage in person, at his return he had better know who his aunt is, how old and how likable she is, what she looks like, the place he met her, how long it took him to go, and the experiences he had, just to stay in the play's plot logic when we see him again. This technique of staying with the scene is what we call "playing the play backstage."

When an actor exits the stage, there will be a certain measure of unresolved tension. The play may be moving on a progressive course at a rate of so many "miles a minute" when he leaves. While he is off backstage, the play receives a booster shot of impulse and progresses faster or slower as the logic of the confrontation dictated. By the time he returns, the play has traveled on to another town, as it were. If he hasn't been intellectually traveling with it, he may quite likely return on a retarded and unrelated speed which is not only discernible to the audience, but may be confusing and upsetting for the on-stage actors.

Some entrances are posited on the resultant reactions of a terrifying event recently committed offstage. Imagine what Oedipus has to achieve mentally and physically before he moves onstage after he's blinded himself. Think of what Medea has to create to come on after she's murdered her children. The actors have to play the play via their own methods of work offstage before they enter to advance the scene with positivity and the believable quality able to engender the classic emotions of pity and fear.

If an actor can learn to play the play offstage, study his entrances and exits and position himself for his next entrance physically and emotionally, he is directly making the best constructive use of his offstage time. The intended release of ideas and action only comes when he has played the whole play by moving into the new key designed by the playwright with every entrance, then moving into yet another, aiming for the end of the play from the beginning.

Time and again actors who write about acting choose the metaphor of getting on a "train" of events and going somewhere—and being sure that if it is necessary to "get off," managing to "get on" again. The constant goal is to progress the plot and arrive at new and logical places, not just maintain the status quo. It is most supportive to the actors' progression when the costumes, makeup, props, sound effects, stage settings, and lights are "going somewhere" too, in terms of the change of seasonal moods, both indoors and out, times of day and night, change of locales, and so forth. Many of these changes are smoothly facilitated by the revolving stage, jackknife stages, wagons, and the clever designing of multiple sets. These progressions are clearly requested or more subtly inferred in the script. They are to be seen as a process of arriving at a new place, giving the audience a fresh visual and emotional focus.

One asks, inasmuch as the basic set may remain the same, how it can be altered to achieve the "someplace else." The playwright invariably has a good deal to say by way of notes on direction. As the actors are moving in time, certainly we are moving in the stage space-place. In the time scale of the play, be it two hours, two years, or two decades, a clear progression needs to be demonstrated logically and colorfully.

When we come to leave a scene, the critical point is not to take the scene with us. We may have been responsible for a relatively important, affecting moment, and then have to exit. By what our body says ("This is not an ending—they will continue without me!"), by the nature of how we move off, focusing the scene behind us, the scene will continue with even greater power after we have exited because the intelligence of it clearly required a progression. The exiting actor should properly phrase and time the lines to allow the attention to shift away from her toward the onstage center of interest.

To keep the level of appropriate awareness, the actor may employ quite subtle movements, such as begin to take a step or two out before the actual exit. Whether she's leaving by her own volition or whether she's been asked to leave, she may commit her intention to exit to the audience before it actually occurs, and it will perhaps not seem quite so abrupt. She may take another step or two towards the door. And then, when she actually goes out, she will probably have her back to the audience, so the scene seems to be left with the people on stage.

A selfish actor might exit by turning toward the audience, looking over her shoulder, then walking to the door, looking again, opening it, and going out, taking the scene with her. That is but another form of grandstanding the exit rather than melding it so that the scene is left onstage for other people to take over. There are exits that *should* be grandstand; very often in farce and melodrama, we time them for that intent and effect. We study that the left hand is available to open a left stage door. We open it up, step through, change hands on the knob, make a speech, and close the door on the next beat, much like we are playing the finale of a piece of music. Often the playwright has given us the words in finale rhythms appropriate for the last act, which may be both the act finale and the play's completed ending.

Recently I directed a student actress in the wonderful nurse's exit in the last act of The Man Who Came to Dinner. I enjoyed discussing with her that after the gross humiliation visited on her by Whiteside, this plotted exit was, in reality, a well-earned entrance, like that of a released prisoner. She was not "making an exit": she was telling off a man who had made her life miserable for some time, and by chance it was necessary to go through a door at the peak moment of conclusion. The minute she played this purpose, it was hilariously funny and structurally correct. In this happiest moment of her onstage life—through playing sheer, fanatic, comic happiness—the real power of the scene was delivered. Such exits are pivotal ones, and may well be considered a hybrid exit—a beginning, not an ending.

Always avoid messy, "oozing" entrances and exits. Too often the timing is slow, because the actor is hearing his cue from offstage when he should have already accomplished all his mechanics of getting the door open and closed, been on to hear and respond to the cue. Many specific, pivotal, important variables surround each entrance and exit and are subject to a due process of analysis, rehearsal, and experimentation in order to approach the exact plotted intentions of the playwright.

Pro and Con

A plot is advanced by alternating issues and actions that are affirmed or negated by the characters, individually and collectively. In working/playing for a total impact on an audience, younger, less experienced actors and directors have a tendency to play the "pros" or the positive emotions more directly and enthusiastically than the "cons" or negative ones, even though it is often more exciting and challenging to play "con" villains than "pro" heroes. The plays I directed that didn't succeed well were in a sense too smooth, too controlled, too "pro."

When the pros and cons have come to the climax of their struggle, one wins and one loses. The victory of the pros tends to signify the comedic side of drama; when the cons win, the tragic and melodramatic element tends to predominate. Often in writing, directing, and acting, the balancing of pro and con is achieved very well, but when one side wins and moves away from the opposition, which is the point when the audience is most vulnerable in its sympathy with the characters, writing and playing can easily become less believable if not carefully thought out, controlled, and presented.

A playwright may build a sense of climax that culminates in chaotic emotions and situations. But as these are resolved, actors tend to become almost instantaneously drained. It then becomes a director's job to maintain believability by retiming the scene carefully, noting how drained the actors are after a major emotional climax, and ensuring that as the rhythm ebbs, the actors don't wash away with it.

This principle becomes very pertinent in many of the tragedies where there are frequent deaths. The greatest ultimate incredulity is to literally overpower the audience—or to convince them to "suspend their disbelief"—with total conviction of death when they know, after all, that the actor is going to play again tomorrow. We achieve that by paying attention to the quality of the "ebb and flow" of an emotional line as it is designed and recorded by the playwright. It is embodied by the actor technically and emotionally. Rather than having to dig repeatedly inside oneself and dredge up the recalled death of a beloved pet or relative to motivate an event of tragedy, it is as effective to cultivate a sensitive awareness of what the playwright has given us to work with creatively to achieve a distinctive and memorable scene.

The Joy of Catharsis

By far the most exciting evening in the theatre came for me with a play which was essentially not considered great, with an acting company which was not at that moment notably prestigious. It was seeing Ethel Waters, the great black actress, who up to that time had been a versatile musical and nightclub singer, play the leading role in DuBose Heyward's *Mamba's Daughters* during the late thirties. She played a courageous mother figure with the most elemental power I've ever witnessed in the theatre.

I have few words to accurately record the experience of her performance. It was transcendent. A few moments after the opening of the play, I had little awareness of being in a theatre. Whatever method the company was employing towards pulling the audience onto the stage, they achieved it with me and everyone else that night. I recall intermissions when I was almost unable to move from my seat. The final climax was one of the most shattering and exhilarating experiences I have known in a theatre. Through the years I've run across a notation here and there about that singular production. The late international director Rouben Mamoulian once said, "I have never seen an acting performance to compare with Ethel Waters in *Mamba's Daughters*." I've talked to actors and actresses who have also felt that this was for them a premier performance.

Not very often does a powerful theatre experience, in which everybody is firmly caught up in a unified structure of simplicity, conviction, and high proficiency, attach itself to what we think of as a less-than-classic play. But this was such a case.

For me, this play was as much a spiritual as an aesthetic experience. The theatre, as it emerged from religious rites and liturgies, is certainly a place for a religious experience to occur, but it may not happen often in one's theatre life, and, when it does, for no known good reason.

Catharsis: what a powerful experience. How strangely satisfying and pleasant it is! How rarely one experiences it—although if one reads Aristotle, one is expected to experience it whenever one attends a well-produced tragedy. In the older classic sense of catharsis, there is implicit joy and exaltation that you escaped the tragedy or catastrophe which has befallen the characters with whom, by the expertise of sensitive planning and portrayal, you become closely concerned. If you were onstage playing the play during a truly cathartic performance, you would probably be aware of a sense of total involvement with the actors and events on stage and at the same time an extrasensory connection out to and into members of the audience.

What you want to communicate is an assurance to an audience or a community: "Here is a theatre experience that I am going to try to bring to you which you have possibly not had before, and it tends to come about through the production of tragedy." Then you hope you have the ability and the talent to deliver it.

On the other side, there is the frivolous play. It's important to laugh buoyantly and brightly about many subjects. But even in the sunniest of comedies, there is a counteraction, a conflict that must be developed, or else the energetic current of action is weakened for lack of conflict. To the good and the happy must come conflicts, confrontations with personalities who taunt the virtues. There must be the vice to set the good in action, to overthrow evil, to triumph in the end.

This contrast is certainly evident as much in comedy as in tragedy, though in tragedy the focus is on those characters who are being torn apart rather than those who are being put together. Since both the rhythms of disintegration and integration are inherent in life, one cannot ignore the value of tragedy as contributing a share of the expression of our existence. Perhaps in a happier world there would be fewer tragedies in the frightening, disintegrating sense of the word; but probably not fewer plays which depict the warm and heroic ways in which people meet and cope with adversity. Their attempts somehow bespeak the indestructibility of the spirit.

The seed idea of catharsis may be extended to all drama, and the joy, pleasure, and delight played out in the performance. The loyal audience comes in willing to suspend disbelief with the trust that the artists in charge know how to help them hear, see, and feel fresh thoughts, ideas, plots and people in moving situations, resulting in believable conclusions, whether bright or dark. The anticipated result is at best to be informed, uplifted, relaxed, and relieved to have escaped the final catastrophe.

What's Entertainment?

The word "entertainment" is often equated with whether a presentation is laughable or at least light-hearted. It is unfortunate that this is the case, because with a paucity of words in describing the many important aspects of theatrical activity, "entertainment" does have a more accurate and broader connotation which comes out of its derivation of *entre-tenere*—"to hold in between." Therefore entertainment implies dramatic or artistic tensions. The audience is entertained when it is held and convinced by the diverse tensions which go into the drama.

An entertaining play contains opposing sides, issues, and characters with various backgrounds and interests who are exploring the playwright's thesis. The playwright gives us the structure of oppositions, and it is our job to be true to the quality of the tensions, to enhance them and clothe them with excitement, humor, and believability. When this tension tends to phase out a bit, it then must receive a new impulse from the actors; if they are successful, the tensions grow to an even larger dimension. The dimensionality of these tensions should hold the audience's interest through the play.

As artists, actors, and directors, we are technicians in accurately sensing, locating, guiding, shaping, and controlling the whole growth pattern of the plot's tensions. We are providing an "entertainment" for the audience—until the climax breaks, and the denouement (which literally means an "unraveling") arrives. Often a director has to maneuver some of the timings at the end of the play, perhaps to hasten it so as not to tarry too long after the tensions have been resolved. The director must exercise judgment as to the audience's credulity at this point how rapidly or slowly the play should be motivated to conclude. Sometimes the director doesn't have all that much help from the playwright to determine this technical decision, especially for her particular community.

When, with a performance piece, it has finished within a certain psychological rhythm and the audience has gone with it enthusiastically, it is, in all probability, entertainment. This is just as true with playing tragedy, which is notable for its holding of excitement, as it is with comedy. One can be thoroughly entertained by the elements of tragedy, which are often more closely related to our deepest emotions, than by the improbabilities of farce or comedy. Classic tragedy entertains because it tends to thrust us into a perspective that is outside of the world we come from. We feel a renewal of an old pulse of pity and fear, a new release which can be immensely refreshing, and which for the last few thousand years is the so-called catharsis.

We are not entertained when we are not held in a planned, organized state of suspense. We get bored when, due to inexpert writing, directing, and playing, there is not a consistent, pleasant, and rhythmic shaping of the tensions. This is true no matter if the vehicle be comic, tragic, or one of the dozens of combinations or even the tens of dozens of hybrids in between.

The Transcendent Quality of Acting

"When all of the actors believe in what they are doing and all members of the audience believe in what they are witnessing, we have all component parts believing something at the same time. The actors believe one another, each actor believes himself, each spectator believes each actor, everyone is believing at the same time. All component parts are in harmony. When all component parts are in harmony, we have the possibility of a work of art—we have unity."
—William Ball, *A Sense of Direction*

The word "transcendence" describes the process by which the play carries beyond the stage and totally into the audience. The audience feels the full power of what is happening. The play is transformed from a inert, mechanical proposition into an organism, with the audience becoming part of the unity of action and reaction.

There is a great warmth, affection, and love about a company of actors who are compellingly alive in a great play, and who are with a receptive audience. In many productions which approach this level, the audience is feeding the actor almost as much as the actor is feeding the audience. It's as though the switch is pushed and the current of all the emotional moments in the play begins to flow.

The audience unconsciously makes warm, encouraging sounds indicating their absorption that can be heard on stage. If the current is not flowing, you hear people cough, feet scrape, and programs flutter; you see people looking down, sideways, and at their watches. When the current is flowing, there is absolutely rapt attention; a quietness so relaxed and warm that if an actor intuitively inserts an extra flick of a finger into what is going on onstage, the audience will record it. So you'd better be sure that flick is a constructive gesture. Every aspect of the production, including lighting, props, makeup, and scene design, contributes to the transcendent effect. Any of these elements out of key with the play will tend to undermine that unity.

As a director, your imagination is engaged when you read a script for the first few times. From then on, you struggle to keep that first impression in your mind, because there are going to be events bombarding you minute by minute that will tend to lower it. You must have the resiliency to counter the situations which tend to change the brilliance of that pristine vision.

The transcendent quality is related to the entertainment factor in tension—that which holds your attention, grasping your interest, love, regard, and belief. Bad plays are boring plays, and the great sin in the theatre is to bore. Boredom is related to the fact that there is no tension there which will hold you.

A memorable experience in the theatre depends on the ability of all the people involved to believe in and to recreate the variable, exciting tensions that have been planted by the playwright to hold the suspense and provide the audience entertainment. This is what takes each member of the audience dynamically and physically out of his or her sense of being in a theatre.

Tragedy is not so different from comedy in its ability to entertain with kaleidoscopic emotional lifts and insights. The fine play, regardless of its mode, has a potential which when realized will give the audience a memorable excitement. It may bestow upon them a brilliant, satisfying ecstasy they will recall many years afterwards.

The memorable impact of a theatrical performance is measured by the level and degree of the response engendered in the audience. There is no *play* until the audience is positively responding to it and accepting it, taking it and holding it.

Seasoned theatregoers, in the process of their lifetime of seeing plays, seem to enjoy viewing life as a stage and all the people as merely players. As a director, I don't consciously attempt to instill that point of view in the audience, but perhaps achieve the same result by taking each play and exploring its particular convictions of a chosen humanitarian thesis in dramatic form. The active presence of the live actors, their mastery of the techniques, dynamically affects audiences informatively, excitingly, and entertainingly.

The theatre experience—speaking now of the live performance before an audience—has in it the implicit, authoritative projection of clear thoughts, clear emotions, and clear actions. The communicative clarity, charm, and sense of well-being, plus the excitement of playing with fine words and phrases when handling the literature of the theatre, make for appreciation, understanding, and conviction. Clarity, in the theatre, is based on a composite sense of joy, proficiency, beauty, spontaneity, and warmth which as an equal response is returned by the audience. It is of value for those possessing degrees of talent, to have that talent disciplined in unaffected presentations of the written word—poetry, oratory, essays, etc., plus the basics of voice production and diction—before accepting major assignments, and being disciplined in turn by the audience. For it is ultimately the audience that tells you whether or not you have been clear in what you're performing.

I try to direct the designers, technicians, and actors towards the concepts that when the production achieves at a maximum level of the company's assembled expertise, the play does not take place on the stage: it takes place in the audience. It is a marvelous conspiracy of the theatre arts, in which an actor measures and expends his energy so it is most surely received by the audience; it is enhanced by the light playing on his face, by the psychological color, line, and mass of his costumes and by his relationship to the other actors in the play as structured by the script. In total, it plays clearly within the strictured modality of the play, whether dominantly comedy, tragedy, farce, or melodrama. The actor sets up an appropriate current of energy with the audience, who are so intrigued by his eagerness, his intelligence, and the clarity of what he achieves, that they understand and respond in kind.

No one has been on the stage in a successful production without having gradually felt the mass audience acceptance. When this current is created and maintained, it rolls back and forth between actors and audience. Once it has been set up, it becomes a professional obligation not to allow the errors which would cut it off—overconfidence, obvious hyper-self-sensitivity which forces important moments of impact inward instead of outward. It's a common experience that when an actor falls prey to this attitude, the other proficient characters on stage sense the faltering in the flow, and revive, revise, and re-energize it to bring the current back again. Probably why closing night performances are rather frequently the best ones is not just that the actors have had more practice in controlling stage fright, but may also be the result of having had more experiences of flow and lack of flow through the preceding performances. The improvement in the contact and flow becomes not only positive but enjoyable.

There must always be within the actor-audience relationship a sense of buoyancy and generosity: "I am an actor because I enjoy it and find that I seem to have an aptitude." Even in the most exacting of deep emotional plays, there should be an uplifting advancing of theme, competently achieved. Plays of deep emotional content often reach, as they probably should, a degree of spirituality. The play is a product of the spirit; it appeals to the whole gamut of bright and dark spirits of the audience and is therefore a spiritual experience. On all levels, from low comedy to high tragedy, the play is made to exist in these mysterious and revealing realms.

SUGGESTED READING

On Acting

Benedetti, Robert. *The Actor at Work.* 3rd Edition. Englewood Cliffs, NJ: Prentice-Hall, 1981.

Bowskill, Derek. *Acting: An Introduction.* Englewood Cliffs, NJ: Prentice-Hall, 1977.

Cole, Toby, and Helen K. Chinoy. *Actors on Acting: The Theories, Tehchniques, and Practices of the Great Actors of All Times as Told in Their Own Words.* New York: Crown, 1949.

Crawford, Jerry L. *Acting: In Person and In Style.* 3rd Edition. Dubuque, IA: William C. Brown Co., 1976.

Hagen, Uta, and Haskel Frankel. *Respect for Acting.* New York: Macmillan, 1973.

LeGallienne, Eva. *The Mystic in the Theatre: Eleonora Duse.* Southern Illinois University Press, 1973.

Meisner, Sanford, and Dennis Longwell. *Sanford Meisner on Acting.* New York: Vintage, 1987.

Olivier, Laurence. *On Acting.* New York: Simon & Schuster, 1986.

Rockwood, Jerome. *The Craftsmen of Dionysus.* Glenview, IL: Scott, Foresman, 1966.

Body Training and Stage Movement

Kline, Maxine. *Time, Space, and Designs for Actors.* Boston: Houghton Mifflin, 1975.

Lessac, Arthur. *Body Wisdom: The Use and Training of the Human Body.* Drama Book Specialists, 1978.

Sabatine, Jean, with David Hodge. *The Actor's Image.* Englewood Cliffs, NJ: Prentice-Hall, 1983.

Direction

Ball, William. *A Sense of Direction*. New York: Drama
Book Publishers, 1984.

Autobiographies

Carey, Macdonald. *The Days of My Life*. New York: St.
Martin's, 1991.
Hart, Moss. *Act One*. New York: Random House, 1976.
Olivier, Laurence. *Confessions of an Actor*. New York:
Simon & Schuster, 1982.
Rathbone, Basil. *In and Out of Character*. New York:
Limelight Editions, 1989.

Dramatic Modes

Kerr, Walter. *Tragedy and Comedy*. Jersey City, NJ: Da
Capo, 1985.

NOTE:

One does not learn to act, or for that matter to be
proficient at any other technique demanded in the wide
ranges of total theatre, by reading books. Every facet of
my education at the Northwestern University School of
Speech in the twenties was a hands-on experience, sensitively applied by highly talented directors, actors,
designers, music and sound composers, and critics.

My personal bibliography was in the form of some
thirty to fifty notebooks which with deep gratitude I
attribute to the grandest old professor I was ever privi-
leged to know, Theodore B. Hinckley. He insisted that
one of the most viable and helpful texts one could have
was a daily account of one's convictions, of what we feel
we have freshly learned and used. He firmly directed
that each page have a vertical line drawn down the center: the left column headed PRO and the right CON.

This applied to lectures, readings of plays and adjunct materials, acting performances, interviews, and conversations.

Most of the "ideas" advanced in this book were experimented with, tested and retested with real living and breathing audiences, and then advanced to students over several decades. Students' responses have dictated the broad and somewhat simplistic topics included here.

Many supportive texts, some of which are listed above, have also been of help to me in re-evaluating my convictions. They reaffirm points I have made herein and cover many other topics as well.

INDEX

Abba, Marta, 26–28
Aesthetic distance, 127–128
"After the fact," 102–104, 105–108
Age, portrayal of, 26
Air, 8, 131–134
American Association of Community Theatre, 6
Amram, David, 45
Appia, Adolph, 11
Aristotle, 142
Audience, 11, 70–71, 117–118, 120–125, 142, 143–149
Audience-centered plays, 128–131
Auditions, 41–42, 46, 49–50, 59

Ball, William, 6, 145
Beginnings and endings, 88–90, 131, 134
Belasco, David, 126
Believability, 53, 79, 123
Black Hills Playhouse, 6
Blocking, 62, 67, 68
Breakthrough, 8–9, 33–37

Cain Park Theatre (Cleveland), 6, 27
Carey, Macdonald, 6
Carnegie Tech, 6, 80
Casting, 43–46
Catharsis, 141–143, 145
Chance-taking, "safe," 37, 80–81, 94, 103, 120
Chekhov, Anton, 79, 126
Clichés, 26, 53–56, 95–96
Climax, 92–96, 134, 140
Comedy, 104–106, 146–147
Constructivism, 85
Crowd scenes, 94

Dalcroze Eurythmics, 11
Davis, Miles, 91–92

Dean, Alexander, 75
Dimensionality, 76–80
Dock Street Theatre (Charleston), 6, 122
"Door" metaphor, 13, 98–102, 107
Duse, Eleonora, 33
Deval, Jacques
    Tovarich, 26

Ears, 48, 58–61, 69–70, 71–74, 82–84, 91
Easton, Hazel, 34–35
Egoconcentrism, 77, 97–98, 121, 130, 148
Elephant Man, The, 107
Emerson, Faye, 6
Emotion, 31–32, 86–87, 149
Empathy, 127–128
Energy levels, 32, 80, 82, 89–90, 92, 93–94, 113, 124, 134
Entertainment, 143–145, 146
Entrances and exits, 27, 134–139
Equus, 107
Evans, Edith, 105
Externalization, 68–71, 79
Extroverts, 18, 72

Feet and footwork, 25–28
Fight scenes, 95
Film acting, 70, 129
Floor exercises, 21–24
Fonda, Jane, 73
Frontality, 129

Gielgud, John, 82, 105
Graham, Martha, 86
Grand Rapids Civic Theatre, 6
Greek tragedy, 86, 128, 136

Hart, Moss, 104
Hearing vs. listening, 30, 71–74
Heyward, DuBose
    Mamba's Daughters, 141–142
Hinckley, Theodore B., 111–112, 152
Holbrook, Hal, 97

Ibsen, Henrik, 126
    Peer Gynt, 5
Instrument, self as, 17
Introverts, 18
Iowa, University of, 6

Julia, 73

Kalamazoo Civic Theatre, 6

Le Gallienne, Eva, 33
Lighting, 130
Logic of humor, 105–106
Luce, Claire Boothe
    The Women, 43

Ma, Yo Yo, 119, 120
Mabie, E. C., 6
Maharishi International University, 6
Mamoulian, Rouben, 141
Man Who Came to Dinner, The, 138
McPartland, Marian, 45
Meisner, Sanford, 46
Memorization, 68–71, 132
Metaphors, 12–13
Method acting, 18, 31
Metrical recitation, 35, 36, 58
Miracle Worker, The, 107
Modes of drama, 93, 148
Molière, 129
Morris, Mary, 80
Mr. Roberts, 95
Muncis, Jan, 11

Newhart, Bob, 6
Northwestern University School of Speech, 5, 9, 34, 52, 88,
    111–112

O'Brien, Pat, 6
Olivier, Lawrence, 115
One Hundred Years Old, 118
Ongoingness, 90

Oppositions, 8, 61–64

Parsons College, 6
Peppard, George, 6
Physicality, 7, 20, 25–28, 62, 73–74, 75
Pirandello, Luigi
    Right You Are If You Think You Are, 27
Place, choice of, 29, 64, 67–68
"Platforms," 85–87
"Play," 115–117
Playboy of the Western World, The, 122
Playing areas, 75–76
Playwright, 74, 95–96
    intention of, 19–20, 22, 31, 32, 57, 61, 62, 77, 126, 130
"Precipitative" playing, 119–120
Pro/con emotions, 139–140
Pro/con evaluations, 111–113, 152–153

Rabb, Ellis, 6
Rathbone, Basil, 6
Reacting, 71–74
Realism, 126
Rehearsals, 91–92, 99–101, 107–108, 111
Rhythms, 19, 20, 22, 58, 127, 132–134
Robards, Jason, Jr., 30

"Saying," 50–53, 56, 84
Scene transitions, 135
Script as impediment, 8, 46–49, 69
Sensitivity, bodily, 21, 23, 24
Shakespeare, William, 53, 107, 124, 128–129
    As You Like It, 90
    Taming of the Shrew, 100–102
Shaw, George Bernard
    Candida, 34
Sheridan, Richard Brinsley, 122
Skinner, Otis, 88, 118
Simon, Neil, 79
Sitwell, Edith, 52
Stage-centered plays, 126–128, 130
Stephenson, Henry, 52
Suspension of disbelief, 124

Taylor, Laurett, 72
Tempo, 105
Three Men on a Horse, 68
Thurber, James, 121
Tragedy, 142–143, 144, 146
Transcendence, 145–146

Underplaying, 83
University theatres, 10

Voice, 17, 28–30, 50–51

Ward, Winifred, 111–112
Waters, Ethel, 141
Wayne State University, 6
Wilde, Oscar, 42
    Importance of Being Earnest, The 69, 105
Williams, Tennessee, 126
    Glass Menagerie, The, 72, 130
Wood, Grant, 6, 131

Yankton College, 6

LaVergne, TN USA
09 April 2010
178722LV00003B/77/A